MW00749641

Formosan American

Memoirs of a Taiwanese American Family

From Pirates To Taiwan Semiconductor

Copyright © 2003 James Yu

ISBN 1-59113-310-6

Published by James Yu, Portland, OR, USA.

All rights reserved. No part of this publication may be reproduced, stored in a retrieval system, or transmitted in any form or by any means, electronic, mechanical, recording or otherwise, without the prior written permission of the author.

PRINTED IN THE UNITED STATES OF AMERICA

Booklocker.com, Inc.

2003

Formosan American

*Memoirs of a Taiwanese
American Family*

From Pirates To Taiwan Semiconductor

By

James Yu

To my Wife, who gave me everything that I needed to live.

Contents

Prelude

At the core of Chinese lies the heart of an atheist. The search winding ever inward, inhabiting the Middle Kingdom apart from heaven and earth. It is the heart of a Buddhist, an ancestor worshiper, a Daoist, a Confuciust, a Muslim, or even a Christian? Ironically, Dad became a Christian after 74 years of pragmatism and only after returning to Taiwan for good. He said he "had to," that there was "no future" for him otherwise even as it has not changed him. It's tough to teach an old dog new tricks.

In the mish-mashed altar of our family shrine where are the borders drawn? Who were the oranges and incense really for? What seemed most important was not to piss anyone off, to cover our bases so to speak. Ambiguity has always been a useful survival mechanism. It was on my mind on this journey as well. How cruelly, crystal clear my brain was working.

Rhythmic jolts and pounding finally stopped after twelve hours of unpaved ditches and gullies. *In Nepal this is called the East West Highway.* Twelve hours of knees knocking on the unforgiving diamond plated stainless steel backing of the Indian steel tubing bent into seat frames. Twelve hours of torturous Hindi music sounding like the squealing of mice at the slaughter. Twelve hours to wonder who I am, where I'm going, and why I wanted to come so badly to this land of sicknesses with no antidote, land before plumbing, land of poor drainage, or much, much too good drainage? The marathon ride strips perception to the bone. The epidermis pealed away like orange reveals my soft vulnerable sinewy fruit.

The bus stopped at the end of the road in the ancient city of Gorkha. Gorkha is the famed birthplace of the rugged mountain men that the British employed as mercenaries in so many of their wars. My ears chime from the ride from Kathmandu and my knees are beaten. The seat over the left rear wheel, softened by shock absorbers made of stone has bruised them to the color of pomegranates. Cruelly, the leg aisles of the bus are half the size of Western buses. I am wedged between two men scented with the home brewed aroma of roxy, fallen asleep on my shoulder. I am an obvious pillow, an unrighteous cow eater. A big, fat, American pillow wedged in too tight to escape.

With my body imprisoned my mind races. It is the only thing I can exercise and I begin by pealing away the masks behind which my own face lives. *In this sense, I am tragically Chinese.* I taste the earthy flavor of our long journey from the fines kicked in the air by the monster truck sized tires that cake my hair and tongue. The center of my being cries to get out of this torture chamber but the passengers up front confound my desires. They take their sweet time collecting their bags, farm animals, vats of yogurt, produce and relatives with no more urgency than if they were picking the ubiquitous yellow mustard flowers for their curry.

Finally, I taste the liquid oxygen of the moist fresh morning air of the mile high foothill town on the Himalya. What the heck am I doing out here? I was surfing Morro Bay and girl watching California blond bombshells in thong bikinis just a few months ago. But at home I could only see half a reflection in the mirror. Will I find the other half by embarking on an adventure? The fresh air is just the elixir I need to clear my throat, and I drink it in with large gulps. I have never thought of air as food. I am a starved Chitwan tiger.

A starved tiger makes a bad glutton convulsing on a hairball. The fresh air proves too pure for my contaminated muscles and I hack away in loud guttural spasms of mud caked spitballs. They eject involuntarily. Now, in front of all of these strangers, I look the fool I have always felt I am. Toweling my shame away, and with my breathing restored, I spy the trail that will take me to my post. It begins above the town bazaar and winds its way for fourteen hours to a place I will call home. Home has always been a question to me; do I really have one? I do not even know where I will stay after my fourteen-hour trek? It may end simply under a tree. My post is accessible by foot or helicopter and I do not have a helicopter. Who will rescue me if I get hurt? This question I know the answer to. I surmise that a cup of dhude chia, (milk tea), is in order to build up my reserves for the trek of my life, out into my future, out into the Himalya.

I allow myself fifteen minutes rest on a wooden bench over a mud floor and tree branched roof pisal, (shop). With the length of my trek it is all I can afford and I smack my lips, snap on my pack and head for higher ground. Starbucks will never duplicate the ambiance in a third world teashop. The tea was excellent and the taste of cinnamon lingers in my mouth.

My marching orders come from Peace Corp Nepal. They instructed me that a bridge engineer is required to assist the Swiss Helvetica's to design and construct a suspended bridge. It will span over a gorge in the western hamlet north of Saurpani. When completed, walking time from adjacent villages are expected to be cut by three to five hours. As I ascend the trail I take mental notes of how construction materials will be carried in on this single-track trail. The nearest hardware store is in India. I wonder how far the steel cables will have to span the gorge, and how they are going to be carried in on this trail that drops into unknown depths? The weight of 30 meters of 1" diameter cable weighs 3 to 4 pounds per foot and is not a job for a single man. An animal will fare no better on this trail. My guess is that the cable will have to be unreeled and chain ganged in over mountains and dales. In some locations the grades are well in excess of 100%. I file my thoughts and push on forward and up. I will gain several thousand feet of elevation before the day is through

fix

and I make sure to focus my attention on the thin scar in the vegetation to preserve life and limb.

Ten hours pass by in the blink of an eye. Time evaporates and stagnates in equal proportion depending on the task in these ancient valleys. While on the trail it floats away. The alpine scenery is humbling and as the clouds peel away they reveal glimpses of the western Himalya like giant fingers on the horizon. Nepalese have always felt the clean lofty heights of the mountains to be the home of the gods. It is a natural assumption.

I wonder if I will feel at home in the land of the gods or will I impassively pass through just another gate in my life? The sky is bluer, the air is cleaner and I feel incredibly buoyant although my limbs are throbbing from the trek. Still well below tree line, I stop below a banana tree to eat some pineapple biscuits bought for five rupees in the bazaar. The banana tree reminds me that I am still at the latitude of Florida even though the extreme elevation of Nepal creates an alpine setting. With the warmth of food metabolizing in my stomach I do feel at home here in the mountains.

Such solitude is intoxicating. The crunching of cookies in my mouth is all that concerns me in the world. From my perch above the river valley below I can see that the trail steeply winding its way down and back up on the other side to an elevation slightly above where I am sitting munching on my biscuits. Across the other side of the valley the trail follows the spiny ridge of the mountains beyond scaling up above to a location beyond sight. Meditating on my food, I consciously reduce my heart rate because the next leg of the trek will be strenuous with a long heavy down and a long heavy push up.

I greedily gobble up the last of the creamy pineapple filling flavored biscuits. I lick every last morsel off my dirt stained fingers, and I sit with my eyes closed for another minute. Just before my body decides to never move again, I skip down into the abyss of the valley like a goat trailing side to side to control the speed of my descent.

Three hours later I summit the crown of the trail at the beginning of the ridge. It is the neck of the spine, which I saw from the other side of the valley beneath the banana tree. I breathe a long sigh of relief and suck in air with my hands on my knees and my head nearly between my legs. The wind is howling on this side of the valley whipping my black hair sharply against my face. My hair cracks angrily against my cheeks that are already red from the effort. I feel lightheaded after my steep ascent, as the air is thinner at about 3000 meters above sea level. In a child's pose, I rest racked over with my eyes closed to the pain. It takes more than a moment until the cobwebs start to clear and for my heart to jump back into my chest from my temples.

When I decide to regain my posture I move slowly and feel the rush of blood to my toes. I open my eyes and all I can see is the abyss of white. My god, I'm blind. I rub in a panic to get the blood back. I blink at the blob in front of my face. Now I see ghosts? A bearded ghost that moves, he jolts me back to reality. His pruned face an inch from nose to nose. It is the dark piercing eyes of a hirsute mountain man with hollow caves for eye sockets.

I yelp like a wounded puppy stumbling over my feet.

The stranger reaches to grab with a stringy chicken claw but its too late. I trip over my pack and cartwheel down the trail. I think I'm dead.

It is the end of my adventure before it begins. So much for me finding out what lies beneath the masks I wear and why they suffocate.

But I stop. I stop to suffer another day.

I stop perched on the precipitous edge of the trail I just spent the last two hours staggering up. I can see the rocks below where my body should be dashed to a thousand pieces.

I laugh.

What a strange animal he is. He stares *at me* like I'm the crazy one. A whole country full of people with little concept of personal space, where women walk arm in arm and men walk arm in arm, but not a man and women. Even they understand that kind of proximity. The hairy apparition rolls his eyes behind the scarf he has wrapped around his head and mouth. His eyes are piercing black daggers lancing right through me. No longer amused with my brush at death, I want to strangle this old goat but I see he is armed. Sheathed on his belt is an ancient sickle knife called a chuchuri. Did he intend to rob me in my weak moment with a quick jab to the throat? His weapon is perfectly suited for the task.

In my best Nepali I ask, "kahaa bouta annu bayo?" which I think means, "where did you come from?"

He shakes his head from side to side, which I have come to learn, means okay or yes. What does "yes" have to do with anything? I ask him again to state his business.

The hairy apparition speaks. "Tapailei tick cha ki china?" he says, "Are you well or not?" He thinks I can speak Nepali. Or does that mean are you crazy or not?

Instinct compels me to shake my head no, no no.

But no is yes, so now it's his turn to shake his head.

"What yes?" I say in English. What are we agreeing on?

"Kati lackcha?" he asks pointing to my watch, which means, "how much does that cost?"

I cover my wrist with my other hand. I have a sneaking suspicion he would have loved to see me dashed to pieces.

"Bhia, tapailei na-ramro dechincha," he said.

You would look ill to if you were just killed, I think.

"I'm not ill," I say in Nepali.

He shakes his head from side to side again which means "yes" in Nepali or "no" in English.

"What are you doing here?" he asks. What am I doing here, what are you doing here I think?

"Little brother, where did you come from?" he adds. I notice he is barefoot and dressed in short pants and a multi colored vest made out of Terratoom fabric.

"I am an American and I have come to help build a bridge north of Saurpani," I trumpet mechanically. I have practiced this speech a million times just for this occasion.

He looks at me doubtfully.

"Japanese?" he says.

"No, no, no. I'm an American," I repeat.

"Japanese!" he says again.

At least I know my language skills are working. Weeks and months of intensive cultural sensitivity training, language training, role-playing and family-stay are paying off. I can communicate at least at a fifth grade level.

"I came from the other side of the valley. That is why I looked sick," I said.

He shakes his head from side to side but his eyes never move or blink even in the howling wind. His eyes say "whatever you say crazy Japanese boy."

"What is it like on the other side of the valley?" he says.

I think I understand him perfectly, but my reflex is to say, "please say it again slowly," to confirm.

"What....is....it.....like.....on........the.......other......side...... of.......the....... valley?" he says again.

What is this some sort of test? Okay smart-ass I think. But I am pretty sure I heard him right for the second time. What is this old fox trying to pull?

I inquire as formally and politely as I can muster, "you have never been to the other side of the valley?" with extreme doubt.

"Of course not," he says eyes unflinching. *"Only a fool travels in another man's country-where he does not know the custom and is not wanted."*

Our Dao (*Our Way*)

I wrote in my son Eli's baby diary along with the impressions of his feet and palms:

Eli, you should know that grandma is crazier than Hunan chicken served over a bed of brown rice. Your grandpa is like pot-stickers served with ketchup and French fries in a Styrofoam receptacle. The contradiction is what killed them. This is why they are not a part of your life today. That is the only shame of their legacy.

Eli is shrimp with lobster sauce, risotto, and shepherds pie all wrapped up in one, a tastier meal than any of us before! When he was one, he would eat pickles dipped in strawberry yogurt, flavors I can not even stand and I grew up on a steady diet of smelly cabbages buried in the ground and the hearts of chickens sautéed with spinach. His palette appears to be tolerant of spicy and mild, hot and cold, plain and flamboyant. He eats them all with such ease and happiness. No plastic packaged meals or food served from a cardboard box will satisfy his diverse appetite.

The Dao, (the way) of Eli's home is built on the flavors that run through him and his unborn contemporaries. But he will need to understand the recipe of how he came to be, because those before him forgot the Dao. Those before him lost the recipe and wandered this land like the ghosts of our dead ancestors. They are still wandering. They are the eccentric dead ancestors of the Yu and Yeh. For his Italian, Irish, and English roots he will have to ask Lynn someday. I can only tell him about the land of Taiwan, the land of the "terraced bay."

Mom was born Chao-Ying Yeh, or Yeh Chao-Ying in Chinese where the surname comes first, in the south of Taiwan. She was born in the city touted as the original cultural capital of the island named Tainan. Tainan was the first major trading center on the island where the Dutch had originally laid the foundations of a colony. Among her many talents, her capacity to leave an indelible impression on people proved to be her most prominent gift and curse. She is the primary reason for all my years of suffering, and conversely, all my feelings of ancestral pride. As far as I have tried to run away from her legacy and from our past it is all too evident that it is alive in me. Reinventing myself has only blossomed into a partially successful experiment. Even my venture into the Peace Corp didn't reinvent me. I have learned it is useless to try to reinvent 5000 years of history. You cannot pull it off without needing to slit your wrists along the way. China and Chinese history has defied reinvention and perhaps, that is why it has endured for so long. Some call it stagnation, but it is what it is, and it is certainly more than a simple word.

If I could not reinvent myself in America as an ABC, (American Born Chinese), my mother surely could not either-especially since ABC is a poor description for what Mom always insisted we were. The impression she usually left on people was the impression she left on my friend Finey during the sixth grade and that was "craaazy man...., crazy squaw." Those were the first words that dribbled out of his mouth when he saw her at the old Safeway.

In 1977, I had thought that the best part about moving to Pasadena, California was that no one knew us out there. But that never lasted for long. Mother could not stand to be without an audience, whether they loved her or hated her. She was truly famous wherever she went and we were left in her celebrity's wake. I was eleven years old when we moved to Pasadena, California from the Bronx, New York.

"Isn't that *your mom* over in the parking lot?" my new friend Carlton Muessman asked.

It always is and I cannot bear to look. He knows it is her, anyway, why make it easy for him?

"Who is that Indian dude with her?" Finey asks.

The Indian dude is my older brother in short, short cut off Levis. His brown chest and belly project beyond the undersized unbuttoned jean vest evaporated by too many quarters cranked up to high heat. His Apache, black mane of hair is rolling around in the wind trailing him like a cyclone, and his brown skin glistens in the sun. He is a Chinese Village People person. A great fit for the streets of Greenwich Village or Berkeley, California.

In my mind, this is not my family. To have them is far, far worse than the life of an invisible Asian immigrant. Mom was too famous in her own mind to be content with invisibility. I longed to be the innocuous janitor, the invisible garbage collector's son. I knew my new friends had family problems of their own, binding us liked a deprived gang, but this was a little too much to share, too soon. Edwin Finey's mom beat him with a belt as if he had been the reason for his father abandoning the young black woman with three kids, and Carlton's German father had slept around on his Japanese mother for years before she demanded a divorce. It left her with two mouths to feed on her own. I thought I would be happy to trade with them on any given day. At least their family shame happened behind closed doors. My family's shame has always been a public form of entertainment. It has always spilled over onto public squares, sidewalks, airports, and bus stations. This is where my father and mother departed from their ancestral traditions where they should have clung murderously to them.

My new California buds Finney, Carlton and I live on Raymond Hill where all the broken, divorced families, and young empty-pocketed singles lived. Playboys, empty bottles of Johnny Walker and diapers spilled over the trash bins in the sea of apartments. The buildings all have astro-turf courtyards and the obligatory palm tree, ivy landscaping. Having escaped homelessness in the Bronx, New York this is paradise. On Amberwood Drive, I play street football on asphalt as wide as the Rose Bowl, and swim in private pools that have low fences easy to jump. For a heartbeat, I float illegally in a private pool. No way I'm going to admit to anyone that those freaks in the parking lot are my kin. I want my illusion of normalcy. I want my own private Pasadena where every apartment complex on the hill is a theme park. *"Come spend your nights at Tikki Terrace, the rent is cheap and the walls are thick."*

The walls aren't thick enough when I hear Finney's blood curdling screams while his mom is whipping the life out of him. I'd come back later, after his mom had passed out from the fit, to see if he wanted to play hoops, and he always did.

But my charade would end that day on Fairoaks Avenue after just four months. It ended when we passed by the abandoned Safeway grocery turned litter box for birds on Fairoaks Avenue and everyone realized it was my fault. It was time to take my medicine that day walking home from Junior High School.

The old Safeway was finished with sand colored California stucco but no one could tell with all the white and black bird excrement caked over it's thirty foot concrete block walls. When Mom and Rup were out, the sun over Pasadena would be paled by the swarming shadow of a hundred fifty million pigeons descending like an ancient plague. The three of us, which must have appeared as dots to the pigeons, and the dark traffic below stopped to stare as the sky above swam like a huge sinister, undulating sine wave. Wild pigeons simply go wild over three-week-old bread bought off the sale racks from Albertson's at 15 cents a loaf. Mom was a wild animal philanthropist. She fed us the same grain and we were pretty crazy about it ourselves.

Mommy was a traffic stopper when she hurled fists full after fists full of free bread into the air to the frenzied mass of pigeons above. Feeding time at shark reef. It was an awesome sight. My brother Ruppert stood next to her in back of a shopping cart full of bread and launched three loaves at a time with his bigger hands. The screeching of the aviaries instinctively mad and competing for free bread was deafening. The two of them are caked in white and black from head to toe. But, they wear grins from corn ear to ear. I know I will never see so many pigeons in so little a pocket of air space ever again-it is wholly unnatural.

My mother is the new bag lady of Fairoaks Avenue. She is the uncontended master of the Safeway pigeons. I don't think anyone will ever break her record. It is impossible to explain to two eleven year olds. It is impossible for me to understand at eleven.

In America, mom is a "crazy squaw," a baglady that can barely feed her children but spends exorbitant amounts of money on pigeons, and I am the son of a baglady. That makes my son Eli the grandson of a baglady. But this is only in America. No one is born into this world a baglady, and Eli's grandma, my mother was born the daughter of a man who could boast his ancestor was a Taiwanese King. In the absence of the kind of notoriety she was used to in Taiwan, Mom would accept the role as queen of the pigeons.

Mom was born the direct descendant of Kuo-Hsing-yeh who Chinese historians consider to be the first Chinese King of Taiwan. Her father was mayor of Tainan and lived in a big fancy Japanese styled house on land passed down for four hundred years. Generations of peasants worked her family's land locked into a feudal existence of servitude as virtual chattel. She, herself, was educated in the finest universities of Taiwan, Japan, and the United States. She is fluent in at least five languages speaking Taiwanese, Mandarin Chinese, Japanese, English and Italian. Indeed, she was gifted within some hemispheres of the mind, yet not a shred of Western style sensibility tingled between her fair dimples.

The material poverty we suffered was felt greater by Mom for having known the Imperial wealth of another age. It colored everything she did, and we were wounded by the kind of torture that only an adoring mother can dish out to loving sons and daughters when she thinks she is doing the right thing. So broken I have been that the self-mutilation of my most essential substance became my only salvation. *It is a remarkably familiar Chinese theme.* We set about reinventing ourselves on a daily basis.

James Yu

When I was a child my mother governed my existence. As such, the duality of extremes ruled my universe. Everything hot and cold but never temperate. The opposites of yin and yang, such as, male and female, heaven and earth, wealth, and abject poverty was not a metaphysical concept but a life threatening reality. The journey from Spring was to find the middle, to find the Dao. It has been my path to spend the rest of my life picking up the pieces. Composing them into a picture I can stand for more than five minutes without the compulsion to shatter them into another million fragments.

I am still the boy who stood outside the A&P in 3 feet of snow begging old women to carry their groceries home for a tip. I am still the faceless dark brown boy at the freeway off-ramp selling oranges on Christmas day as strangers sit trying to avoid my eyes. I am still the boy who slept on Lake Avenue on Valentine's Day waiting to sell flowers to lovers in big shinny cars who had somewhere to go besides the cold finality of the street. The only difference today is that I have left the shame behind.

On Lake Avenue in Pasadena, I can still remember seeing Jane Sheridan waving at me from the back of her big shiny black SAAB, but I don't want to believe someone from my homeroom class has seen me. Her white mom and dad are dressed in shiny holiday outfits and must be taking Jane to a festive party. I imagine lots of loving relatives and rich tasty foods. It looks warm and cozy in her luxurious, leather-lined car. I try to think up excuses in my head as to why I would be lying on the cold concrete roadside like some drunken, sour smelling, homeless bum.

But it's no use this time even though I have become an accomplished tale weaver by seventh grade. This will be impossible to explain away. I will never have a life like Jane's life. I will never have a date with the likes of a girl like Jane, so clean and white. No dirt under her fingers, no ink stained x-ray imprinted palms from peddling newspapers. I laid my small, soft head back down on the pavement and stared at the gray December sky. It is so ridiculous with the palm trees waving around in the wind during the season of

21

giving. I've been pushing holiday roses for six hours straight without a bathroom break and my hunger pains are getting confused with the need to urinate. I wonder where the hell the van full of round and sweaty, Russian child labor bosses are that's supposed to pick me up? They are making a killing off black, Mexican, and Asian urchins like me. Sales are getting slow as the darkness creeps in and the headlights of the cars blind me as they pass. My eyes slowly close and I fade off to the luxury of darkness where I imagine I am equal with the likes of Jane, and it is hard to pull me back to the light.

It is still hard on days to pull me back. The ironic part of it is that *I have spent nearly my entire life trying to hide the past, but not surprisingly it won't die.* Of course the past is me-almost as much as the future. But it's the new millennium and time for the hunchback to come out of the basement. The time is ripe and as the Daoist say "the hero makes the era and the era makes the hero". Our clan's story is not about *who is right or who is wrong, it is simply about what we have needed to do to survive and I have come to accept there is little shame in that.*

Taiwan

Mom always said, "you are not Chinese, you are Taiwanese!"

That was confusing to me. *What is the difference and why should anyone care?* Why care indeed? The question begs why anyone should care about world peace as well? Can there be stability in the world if 1.2 billion people wish otherwise? If there is a way, I cannot think of it.

It was easier to think of myself as an American, at age seven, even though at that age I had no idea what that was except that I was born in America. Of course everyone called us "chinks" when we were growing up so that added to the confusion.

"Chink go home!" was a common greeting.

"I'm not Chinese," I would reply, "my Mom says so!"

"Okay, Jap go home!" was shouted back.

"I'm not a Jap either," I would say, "I'm a...., I'm a *Tink* not a Chink."

The altar boys in New York from St. James never appreciated my humor. As a result, youth involved a great deal of screaming and shouting, accompanied by rocks accelerated through the air. I become accomplished at dodging the missiles. The young don't have the velocity to kill but the older kids have been trained by little league. I have to mind who is behind that rock or it is bloody result. I beat a path like a chicken trying to save his head. Its no wonder

Fran Tarkenton is my hero. He is my favorite NFL quarterback of all time. Fran Tarkenton played football for the Minnesota Vikings in the 1970's and some said he had eyes in the back of his head. That is what I needed, eyes in the back of my head.

Today, China says that Taiwan is a renegade province of the ancient motherland and threatens to "cook," the island "with a very big fire," if it should ever declare independence. The reference to culinary preparation is an ancient Chinese metaphor for making war. The communist People's Liberation Army threatened to "bury" American naval forces that rushed to the Straits during the 1996 election that ushered Lee Teng-hui into the Presidency.[1]

Beijing, fearing a formal declaration of independence by Taiwan if Lee was elected in 1996, sought to influence the Taiwanese electoral results by launching missiles along each end of the Island and massing troops along the Southern Coast of China renamed Nanjing Military Zone. In response, the United States sent two aircraft carrier battle groups into the area.[2] The vitriol that resulted printed in *Wen Wei Po*, a Beijing controlled Hong Kong newspaper expressed the extent of the Chinese affront at Western hegemony. "With a concentrated fire of guided missiles and artillery, the People's Liberation Army can bury an enemy intruder in a sea of fire," the newspaper quoted. *Wen Wei Po* reported further that Chinese forces would need less than six hours to mount a successful invasion of Taiwan.[3] Such extreme language can hardly be misinterpreted.

But the Chinese strategy backfired and Lee was ushered in with a landslide victory in the first free democratic, two-party elections in the history of the island. Buoyed by his overwhelming mandate from the people, Mr. Lee said, "Taiwan is Taiwan and always has been," and added on German radio that Taiwan should deal with China on a "state-to-state basis," further aggravating the Mainland Chinese.[4] A Taiwanese activist was quoted by the media saying, "China is just a word." The result has been the creation of a regional arms race across the straits, threatening to destabilize the entire region.

What is China? How does Taiwan differ from China to begin with? Why are so many people arguing about this distinction threatening war and annihilation? The rocks they threaten to sling across the Straits are prodigious. For westerners to have an appreciation of this potentially incendiary dilemma they need first understand the anatomical difference between a Chink and a Tink? I have never met an American in my entire life that has had this ability, or an understanding of my complex ethnicity.

When I stepped off the plane in 1995 at Taipei's international airport I still lived happily behind the multitude of masks that I had grown to protect myself from all these questions. I could be anyone at any given time. Chink, Tink, Mexican, Philippino it did not matter. But who I really was, and where I had come from was suppressed. I had spent too much time molding myself into what I knew people at home in the states were comfortable with. Where is it that my ancestors had come from and why is it that I have been ashamed of it for so long? *What is the anatomy of a Tink anyway?*

As Lynn and I disembark from Northwest flight 685, my olfactory senses are confused and my mind is unbalanced by the assault of unfamiliar oxygen. The feeling is unmistakable when I step off the plane. I am in a foreign land. The weight of the air is heavier, denser as I can push against it and it pushes back. There is more water in the air in the tropics more mana (spirit, energy). Cold weather tourists visiting Hawaii adore this sudden shift of latitude and longitude. My island of Taiwan is brother to the tropics. The land of transistors and cheap trinkets lies in the East China Sea only a few hundred miles east off the southern tip of China. It is a modest stone throw north of the island nation of the Philippines. On a clear day from Kenting beach along the southern tip of Taiwan both neighbors can be spied with the naked eye.

For my wife Lynn, it is her first time in Taipei. She was Lynn Dowlen then and there are no gold bands on our fingers, yet. It was the first time I had been back to visit my ancestral homeland since 1976. A lot of things can happen in nineteen years. Even still, I feel that familiar childhood numb sick feeling in my gut as we find our sea legs on the gangplank off the plane into the terminal. I had hoped to bury that nauseous feeling long ago. The rush of hot, humid, tropical air added to my discomfort as the perspiration found its way to my temples and wet rings formed under our armpits. I am ridiculously nervous for a person on vacation, but here I was to see my father. I am here to reconcile my past and to introduce him to my future.

My father had shrunk since the last time I saw him. The last time we met he stood a modest five feet eight inches tall but it appeared a mere six years had eroded away another two to three inches off his escarpments. Weaned on Big Mac's I towered over him and have since I was sixteen. A man well into his sixties he stood at attention, like the stone lions outside a monastery, grinning as wide as the guardians and impeccably dressed in a fashionable western gray suit. The white hair that ringed the crown of his baldhead contrasted with the dark tan skin of his round Asian face. I thought he looked great and reached to give him a hug. He jerked back, offering a half-hearted response. It was not in him to be physically emotional. Thirty years living in the states did not change him, *and I knew that he was about as American as an Asian immigrant could become.*

After seeing his warm smiles and humble greetings, I begin to feel more optimistic about our visit, but deep down I knew that my father and I barely agreed on anything and 12 days was probably not going to bridge that gap. It was not that we did not understand each other. We understood each other a little too well. I wondered if having Lynn along would keep things civil or limit our conversation to platitudes? For the moment, Dad was being quite charming and we left the terminal smiling and happy. As we sat in the back of the taxi and zipped along the ring road encircling the city at a ripping pace the conversation quieted and I could make out the lights of the city in the distance. Past midnight the streets could barely contain the deluge of vehicles of every size and type from scooters to Mac trucks. I shut my eyes and drifted as my thoughts slipped back to the first time I was in a Taipei cab more than twenty years ago.

1971

From the very first day, I hated Taiwan. To my soft, young, sheltered brown eyes it was a filthy country of open sewers, jet-black smog filled streets, noisy volatile people speaking a strange sounding tongue that manufactured the spraying of saliva when the conversation heated.

"Jesus Christ, stop spitting in my face!" I wanted to scream as my relatives greeted me with strange words of adoration and pinches on the cheek. We were being dumped off at Yu Li-Keng's house, Dad's eldest brother. Twenty-seven hours earlier my older brother Rupert, older sister Rowena and I departed alone and parentless, on a frozen winter morning, from our home on Cambridge Avenue in the Bronx. Dad had to pry my fingers loose from the ice encased wrought iron fence, painted black; to fold me into the waiting yellow bunt cake shaped cab. I went kicking, crying and screaming and I guess I knew this was my baptism into the adult world at five years old. Mom and Dad simply could not afford to feed us anymore. Baby Carolyn lay in an incubator at St. Lukes Hospital near death and rapidly draining away our bank account with every artificial respiration forced into her failing lungs. Endless typed bills smelling of carbon paper ended my father's status as a small shopkeeper of candles, incense, beaded curtains, back scratchers, and Asian imports.

I always loved the perfume scented candles and spice of the incense that flavored the air. Bankruptcy looming, Dad plywooded

27

the windows to his shop on Kapok Street in the Bronx. Dad has always been an idea man, not a nuts and bolts type of Joe. There was no manual for what he needed to understand because what he learned about family affairs was inherited from the old country. No health insurance meant no safety net. But, Chinese do not leave family matters to an outside agency, not even the "good hands" people. Family issues are resolved within the family Confucian model and are not thrown into the public sphere. He would never absorb this lesson and drove for another twenty years in America without insurance. I drove for another ten years without auto insurance. To drive with it would have effectively excluded me from the class of the mobile, as I could not afford it more than his contempt for public assurances.

Our relative's house on my father's side of the family in Taipei, where we were exiled indefinitely, was a mixture of the old and the new frontier Taiwan was evolving into. The industrial transition that was transforming the island in every sector was most apparent in the northern capital in Taipei. On the one hand their house was recently wired with limited electricity, a monumental leap, on the other, it did not have indoor sanitation or plumbing. Even in the 1970's in Taipei, the toilet was a hole in the ground.

A shallow pit like Uncle's smelled like a depository of 1000-year-old sweet and sour pork. Sometimes I wondered if any of our relatives were buried down there? No pressurized flush and no toilet paper are required to operate a pit latrine. Stagnate communal feces tainted water, on the other hand, is required in the operation. Water in an old yellow stained jasmine tea tin collected off the roof to refresh the backside is the preferred method and evolution of the leaf in refreshing the soiled parts. After our combed and shiny novelty was replaced with long destitute scowls, queer looks begin to replace the broad smiles of our hosts.

"How, how, how," meaning, "okay, okay, okay," is heard less, less and less.

No extra serving of dried pork over amoyaa (porridge rice) can bring us out of our morose and self-pity. Nothing they do can compete with air-conditioning, Sesame Street, carpeting, bunk beds, underground sewers, or tree lined streets. It confirmed their suspicions that we are a bunch of spoiled rotten American brats and of course, we are spoiled.

But at five, the immersion into third world accommodations are inexplicable and I am terrified of the pit latrine and of their strange foods and general practices of hygiene. I am instinctively convulsed by what I perceive as dangerous to my well being. Unintentionally, I insult them deeply with every upturned nose. My fear and loathing will not allow me to eat and enjoy freely and every act is a struggle. When they offer me a black-yoked egg with a salt preserved middle I run for dear life. They chase me down.

"Delicious, delicious" they insist as they run me down.

I am soon obsessed with washing my hands and wash them so many times a day that they dried up like two little stubs cracked and deformed with open sores. What they call soap is the same thing they use to wash their clothes, dishes, cars, buildings, and it is actually a form of powerful detergent. It is nothing like Ivory, which would do nothing for industrial grease stains on concrete compared to the Taiwanese sand paper cakes. But I wash, undeterred, to save my life. No one is there to tell me to stop.

A trek to the black, smelly pit is all I need to set me to washing. It also tests my ability to hold my breath, and my gymnastic ability to straddle the huge hole with my tiny, chubby legs. The hole is cut for adults, children having long departed from the home, and a fall would be a horrible drowning. Sometimes as I looked down between my aching squatted legs into the abyss, I wondered why the hole was never filled to overflowing? Where did the poop go? The cold jolt of the standing water in the tin can and the yellow, warm, Jello like diarrhea-softened turds brought me back from my daydreaming. I squished them between my tiny fingers as I swiped my backside and I could draw pictures with it on the ground. The methane-powered odor that rose from the pit kept the temperature inside the small room dizzying.

My untrained squatting muscles twitched away with a buzz and I feared falling in. The fight with the gravity of the pit flavored my forehead with salty sweat. Emerging from every trip to the pit was like rounding the corner of your home block after a long trek to a foreign neighborhood. The rush of fresh, cool air was the reward. As a result, each visit was a fire drill and I didn't get all the cracks and crevices clean.

Twenty-eight days later, I developed a burning rash that cracked the skin on my anus so severely that I could not sit down without leaning on an undamaged cheek. The cuts on my hindquarters measured over an eighth of an inch deep and looked like "cooked skin" my brother said. I kept them a secret until I could not keep it anymore. I did not know how to heal them but I did not want anyone to touch such a personal area either. The itching was horrible. It kept me wide eyed at night and I tore into them with the zest of a crazed, flea-infested dog. They bled and portions scabbed over which brought the itching again. The cycle was renewed over and over again for months. This is my first memory of Taiwan.

It was the first time I would see brown electricity. Spaghetti thin electrical wires littered the streets wrapping around windows, doors and trees with seemingly no regulation. Most houses, as well as ours, were experimenting with the curious invention. Viva la experiments, because at least we had fans! Every appliance store in town stocked fans. Standing fans, short fans, window fans, ceiling fans, windmill fans, hand held fans. Fans saved our lives.

Having come from the dead of winter in New York, the heat and humidity was unbearable and opening a window for relief was offset by a charge of mosquitoes the size of Maine lobsters. Sweet blood drawn from tender arms and legs quickly looked like chewed up swollen piece of beef jerky. Suffocating one day, I dared to open a window and was instantly smashed in the face by a flying roach the size of a football. I thought it was a bird but Rupert and Rowena are screaming and diving for protection. Auntie Huan vaults to the rescue and smashes the huge roach with a broom. Yellow guts and brown shell are splashed about like an exploded watermelon.

"Awlite, awlite" auntie chuckled as she tapped my head, "just bug."

Taipei was a basin for the accumulation of standing water. The variety of fauna developed within the endemic bug kingdom was prodigious. So, we sleep curled in a ball under mosquito netting and the mist of DDT laced toxic coils burned to keep them at bay. After eight months of this routine they wrote my parents, "come get Philip, he is coughing up blood and he is in bad shape."

In the meantime, we remained caged behind the bars of the language barrier. We seldom ventured beyond the safety of our block composed of nothing more than a treeless stretch of concrete buildings with stores lining the road. On short trips with relatives, Taipei proved to be a complete mystery. It made absolutely no sense and watching the deluge of people, taxis, busses, scooters, ox carts, and mobile food vendors zigzagging in every direction was exhausting without an idea of why or where they were all going. We could not read a single street sign nor decipher a single address number. About the only thing I could figure out by talking with my brother and sister was which way was east. I wanted to know which way was home.

We never played with children our own age. They were in school, but we simply melted hour after hour banging our heads against the wall around the house. The one relief from the endless ticking of the wind up travel clock Mom gave us was movie row. On the west side of town, movie row was a lively concrete canyon of twitching blue, red, and green neon. It was my favorite part of Taipei where all the major theaters are crammed within a few blocks. Even more than usual the streets overflow with the damp heat of humanity and the "pang" perfume of freshly steamed bao could make me salivate while I was still on the bus there.

Eldest cousin, Yu Jong-Yuan was an action junky and gathered us to whisk us away from our solitary colorless predicament. Eldest cousin was in High School and he was our hero. I stayed close enough to bump into his knees while walking the streets of movie row. He introduced us to "Revenge of the Flying Guillotine," "Five Deadly Fists," and many other Kung Fu greats. Theaters vied for the attention of the passer by with four-story high hand painted murals of the movie's they were showcasing. Murals featured handsome Que-tailed heroes and heroines from Chinese folklore in outstretched, Wu-shu poses.

No Kung Fu film was complete without warring families and clans tied up in epic Hellenistic struggles. Unbelievable feats of physical stunts and displays of martial arts prowess were simply a must and are always the rice and soy sauce ingredient. We feasted on rice and soy sauce and were always left asking for more, more. Someone's modest, righteous father was inevitably murdered in the plot. His pious son would escape detection by hiding under a farm hat. He would auspiciously fall into the care of an Iron Fist master. Twenty years later, the son rises like a phoenix to avenge the father. We love it; we can't get enough of it. As silly as some of the plots are for these early attempts at cinematography in Taiwan, at the heart of them they reveal the traditional Chinese emotional value of the family and the clan. Nothing is more monstrous than killing a father unjustly. Nothing is more just than an obedient son. It is the Confucian paradigm set in a World Wrestling Federation format.

First run Hollywood films also bathed the silk screens inside the temples along the neon canyon. I saw "The Three Musketeers" for the first time in a gigantic gold painted balcony laced theater with eldest cousin. From the very opening of the movie, which flickered images of close-ups of swordplay in slow motion to the beat of classical orchestral music, I was instantly transported off the island of Taiwan. I left the theater wet around the collar and temples and as exhausted as if I had just endured a transatlantic crossing.

But when we were not delivered to a fantasyland, my bedtime pillow was never dry until the crusted saline of morning. I missed falling asleep against Mom's breast and the sweet musky scent of her pajamas. I missed scratching the sandpaper cheeks of the unshaven face of my father on a Sunday morning while he was trying to read the New York Times. I missed Kentucky Fried chicken and Chunky soup, Mr. Roger's Neighborhood, and The Magic Garden. I drifted off to sleep clinging onto worn out football and baseball cards, crumpled into the texture of toilet paper. I hated this backward, barbaric land and prayed every night for deliverance from its godless shores.

After nine months, my father finally answered my prayers.

1995

There is nothing more tiresome than to always be aware of the singularity of your heritage. Internally I have had to decide how much do people *really want to hear.* Undoubtedly, I have been far too short with those who have a genuine interest and far too lengthy with those who expect a one word response and usually answer the question for themselves by spurting out "Chinese" or "Japanese." In either case, I am dissatisfied with the experience. It is living in a world all my own and in many ways it mirrors China current uneasy relationship with the western powers.

When I look in the mirror it is not the person that my neighbors think they see. No one knows me because there is no understanding of my kind and virtually no understanding of Chinese much less Taiwanese history. Taiwanese compose a very small minority in the United States but every one in five people on the earth has some form of Chinese blood running through their veins and that should be an alarming realization. It suggests the magnitude of ignorance that prevails in our world today.

To learn the craft of making my memoirs into a story, I attended writing seminars, one of which was sponsored by the Oregon Writer's Colony called *Pick me up Tuesdays.* The speaker Bill Johnson, author of *A Story Is A Promise,* was the guest speaker that evening at Borders Books in Tigard, Oregon. As part of the lecture he asked the attending audience of aspiring authors what it was they were currently cobbling and what the essential message of the story was. I explained my work both naively and enthusiastically to the mostly blue-haired gallery, which elicited the response from an elderly man of "who would care about that?"

It caught me off guard and I was surprised to discover that I was surprised by the question. Faced with the stares of writers I presumed to be my better I could not utter a word in defense or explanation. Most of the other's memoirs are about churning butter on the farm, how much harder life was in the old days, how much better life was in the good old days, or how greater the morality of society was in the past. Considering these topics, it was an understandable question. What I remember of the good old days was a lot of people yelling "chink," or "gook" at me, and my view of the halcyon days of the "good old days" are miles from the gentlemen who asked the simple question.

It dawned on me that to write our story I was going to have to flip over my protective shell and reveal my soft underside. It is not something I like to do considering the years of practice I have at lining that very shield. Furthermore, I was faced by the knowledge that the exercise would not even be well received, much less appreciated. However, I see it as all the more reason to tell our story. Recent events surrounding the detainment of 24 American Navy aviators in the South China Sea and the ensuing diplomatic crisis make it obvious that an elementary understanding of China and Asians in general is paramount to peace in tomorrow's world. To have any hope of the future, I have to believe that at least some people will care about the story of Taiwanese Americans.

The fact that the crew of the American spy plane, forced down to Hainan Island due to a mid-air collision with a Chinese fighter plane, was so easily detained by the Chinese government should send alarms and red flags to Americans. Who would have cared about Hainan Island until recently, and an obscure geopolitical struggle between Taiwan and China, so equally far away, may suddenly seem not so obscure when one realizes the values that are under attack. We can kid ourselves and think that the rights of others, however distal, when overrun will have no consequences for Americans.

Whatever China does in the future one thing can be sure. The wake that 1.2 billion people create will be felt by all nations bobbing in its bow waves. Of course, there are high government officials in America who understand this and that is why the spy planes are flying in the first place. They rationalize that East Asia's strategic importance, including Taiwan, justifies the expenditure of American tax dollars to assure that a check on China is necessary. But what does this really mean?

This will not be the last time China and the United States will have disagreements. As such, the response of "who cares" is unacceptable. At the end of each day there are 1.2 billion similar to or like me and they will not stand to be invisible for much longer. They will not be content to be second to anyone and they will not be and that is indeed quite dangerous.

In 1996 when China threatened to invade Taiwan and the United States responded by sending an aircraft carrier battle group to the straits, the unrestrained vitriol launched in the media back and forth from China to the United States was much of the same as today. Although the situation was more intense in 1996 the content of the messages were similar. During the crisis in 1996, each was quick to condemn the other as evil and morally substandard.

The American media settled into a campaign of highlighting the Chinese disregard for human rights, such as the suppression of the Falun Gong, while the Chinese drove home the recurrent theme of the "American threat" or good old western imperialism as a rallying cry to unify the people and power. The communists assert "Falun Gong to be a tool of hostile Western forces, directly nurtured and protected by, among others, the C.I.A."[5]

For many Americans used to thinking of themselves as completely lovable it is a shock at how much Mainland Chinese hate the American government. For the life of them they cannot understand why the Chinese were so stuck on an apology before releasing the 24 American aviators in the past week. Indeed, the official response from Washington was begrudging regret after 12 days and no actual apology. Why should the Chinese be upset with our planes flying in international waters anyway, right or wrong? Many Americans cannot fathom the fanatical extent of Chinese apprehensions concerning hegemony from the outside world. They do not realize how it has been built into the Chinese psyche over thousands of years and what a powerful force it can be in shaping the future of the region. We would be upset too if Chinese aircraft carriers cruised up and down the coast from California to Alaska and sent spy planes so close to our shores to have to elicit a response from our National Guard fighters stationed in Portland, Oregon. But we cannot even imagine the Chinese reaction to such events. The fact that it took so long for our government to issue a simple apology to release our fighting men and women troubles me almost as much as the Chinese insistence for one. It shows a lack of understanding of history and the Chinese siege mentality.

The status quo of usual rhetoric launched back and forth is nothing more than simplistic sound bites, which do nothing to further the understanding of each side and draws the very real problems discussed further and further from a state of mutual understanding. To the credit of both Americans and Chinese, recent events appeared to have been resolved in a relatively cool headed manner given the wide gulf in understanding between the two cultures. We have one thing to thank for this and it is not brotherly love and understanding, it is trade.

Jet lagged and dripping from the humidity, the main thing I remembered from our blinding taxi ride from the airport to my father's flat in Pan Chiao City were the giant K-TV neon lit karaoke bars. The year was 1995 and the Chinese were on the brink of lobbing missiles at Taiwan and reissuing threats of invasion due to the upcoming island presidential election.

Enjoying the calm before the storm, we appreciated the banal prolific architectural application of neon along the crowded boulevards that would put Las Vegas to shame. Neon K-TV letters four stories high. They are appropriately scaled for the Costco-sized bars, which lined the enormous boulevards. The K-TV karaoke lounges are super-sized adult pleasure palaces. The imagination runs wild at the endless titillation's that lay inside a place with that much square footage so boldly advertised on the gigantic concrete tilt-up walls.

My girlfriend, Lynn, and I awoke the next morning to a rain filtered sunny blue skied December day, lifting our spirits like tiramisu having left the steel blue gray of Seattle, Washington. Dad's apartment was a cool spacious three bedroom bare concrete floored cubicle quickly heating up with the rising sun. It was the kind of cell I had spent my exile in on my first trip to Taiwan except twice as large.

The combustible energy and noise rose from the street below gaining strength as the day unraveled. We never had such a spacious apartment like this when we were a family of six. Naturally, I wondered how Dad was financing such grand accommodations? Other than the size, the apartment building is typical in the crowded urban satellite of Taipei called Pan Chiao City.

Taipei suburbs are modern concrete canyons of cliff dwelling urbanites. I could not imagine a time when the first concrete box along the side of a dirt road was built but it was not more than a generation ago. Time and space quickly dictated that there would be thousands of identical boxes stacked up against each other like cigarette cartons as far as the eye can see. The boulevards cut through concrete canyons and are rivers of compacted asphalt. Land is a premium on any island but this is the most densely populated in the world. There are no such grandiose ideas such as setbacks or privacy buffers and buildings are built right up to the property lines in every dimension. The tighter and closer the better. The only exception is the street where concrete gives way to the ribbon of asphalt below.

Underneath all apartment buildings are shops and restaurants often owned or attended to by the inhabitants living above. Almost every building is a mixed-use building embodying a live work situation. The shops below are stocked to overflowing with every type of goods and services imaginable under the warm tropic sun. Taipei is a giant one-stop mega-store. This is the legacy of Chiang Kai-shek and his Chinese Nationalist regime in Taiwan that arrived after World War II. The never ending river of human commerce flows brown and black, back and forwards three hundred and sixty-five days a year, twenty-four hours a day past my father's living room window. Four stories below the torrent rages. Commerce runs so heavily over the embankments of the roads that there is no room for pedestrian walks.

Walkways are patched together, as if an afterthought, underneath the second floor of the concrete boxes sitting above. The columns of the buildings flush out right up to the edge of the roads and form a visual boundary and false sense of security. It is a colonnade between walker and vehicles. The cover is much appreciated shelter for walkers from the winter typhoon. However, walkers spill over into the streets, and merchants spill over into the walkways, and vehicles spill over just about anywhere they please, making a moving broth of uniquely unregulated Asian flavor. Taipei is a Capitalist, Republican, regulation free, business friendly paradise.

My father's living room fronts the street below and sits right over the exterior colonnade elevation. He is sipping Oolong tea above the toothpick columns below and reading the *Taipei Times* as we yawn into the room. We have been sleeping in one of the two guestrooms at the back of the apartment. The rears of the apartments open to an alley, which faces the back of other apartments on the next street over. The back of the apartments are a private world where much of the everyday life of the concrete cliff dwellers happen. The back is where the terraces are, where the laundry is washed and dried, where food is often cooked. It is incredibly quiet within the concrete insulated curtilage setting of the back alley. Clotheslines fly in every direction blowing in the wind like Tibetan prayer flags.

We wake with a case of hemisphere lag. Dad offers tea to warm our stomachs and slippers to warm our feet, as the floor is stone cool to the touch. Rays of sun trickle through white linen drapes. Dad is gracious offering moon cakes and coconut crackers. It is a good start to a sunny day.

"So what are your plans James," he asks?

"I don't know" I say.

"Do you remember Taipei?" he inquires.

"I, I don't know," I say thinking about my surroundings.

"Probably not, eh," he says. I munch on a moon cake. He munches on a cracker.

"I would like to see the Chiang Kai-shek memorial" Lynn interjects. He stares at Lynn. I stare at Lynn.

The coconut cracker slips off the side of his mouth. He fumbles with it as I watch him juggle it.

"Why do you want to go *there,*" Dad asks as he smacks the crumbs off his lap?

"I don't know" I say.

Lynn shows him the travel book where she and I have innocently marked the glossy pages that caught our attention. He looks over the impressive shinny photos of the huge structure and reads the glowing captions. He puts his glasses on to thumb through a few more pages. He seems absorbed by the travel book for the next minute and that is fine with me.

"Kong-dai…" he mumbles under his breath.

"Where else would you like to see?" he says.

It's my vacation I'm thinking. We will go where it pleases us, even if I am making bad tourist decisions. He knows that I was never taught a great deal about the place I had continually professed to have hated and that I had done my best to unlearn what little I knew; I was not expecting to impress Dad. He was not going to make me feel guilty for wanting to fit in at home, but did I really fit in at home and did I fully realize the cost?

"It's your fault," I said in defense.

Lynn says "your very good at the blame game."

Let the games begin.

There was little question that I was guilty of the suppression and mutilation of identifying ties to my ancestral homeland but so were Mom and Dad. The question of '*who they were and are?*' is as great a mystery as my own. Were they American? Were they Chinese, Japanese or Taiwanese, Taiwanese Fukienese, or Taiwanese Haaka, or Taiwanese Ming? It's not my fault that we lived in a world that did not care.

Why did they have to go on chirping about it to people when I could see our neighbor's eyes glaze over at home in the U.S. Why couldn't they have just taught us and kept the rest to themselves? Instead, they tried to make everyone else understand, except their own children, and not surprisingly, they failed. They never understood why it was embarrassing for those of us born on U.S. soil. How dare Dad judge me now for wanting to visit the Chiang Kai-shek memorial?

Dad rubs his chin and stares up at the ceiling as if measuring his response.

It was shameful that by now, *Made in Taiwan* is about as much as I could appreciate about my homeland, and I was virtually starting from scratch. I was here to reconcile this void or remain interminably ignorant. I am determined, like the alarms of a biological clock having exploded, to learn the many faces of Taiwan. I would relearn how my ancestors arrived on the island and how others had migrated to this dynamic island.

In the past, there were precious few things my father and I could see eye to eye on. I was the ungrateful banana, yellow on the outside but white on the inside; returned home to visit a land I knew virtually nothing about. That is what Dad had called me years ago in Los Angeles, the "American banana."

Look who's talking, he was Americanized too except he had adopted all the worst things about western culture, I thought. Now I was going to try to see the world through my father's eyes before there was no more time left to try. I was not completely sure I wanted to see the world from his perspective. However, I realized that his eyes were eminently finite and the time to start looking was now or never. Inevitably even looking through my father's eyes, I would not see the same things.

I was not forgetful of my family's turbulent past and the plan was to spend the first few days with Dad and the last few days with Dad. A dose of Dad in small, easily swallowed, steamed buns was my thought. In the middle Lynn and I would circumnavigate the tobacco leaf shaped island by driving down the rugged eastern coast to the southern tip of Taiwan at Kenting Beach and return up the main artery of the island on the expressway over the western plains. We would give ourselves a week to complete the five hundred-mile tour. This was my plan to learn about my ancestral homeland, my father, and to keep the peace. It was an ambitious plan not fully realized until the year 2001, and it evolves still.

"Drive around the whole island?" he asks. "What for? You have relatives to see here in Taipei," he emphasizes by pausing to sip some tea.

"I...," he says pausing to cup both hands to point at himself, "myself, have never, never even driven around the whole island" he declares. And you are proud of that, I thought?

I can see Dad is doing math in his head. His eye pupils roll to one side of his eyes as if he has a hidden abacus in his eyelids.

"How many days gone?" he asks.

I give Dad sunny answers and explain our plans. I feel like I am six years old again, trying to sell him on the idea and merits of buying me another ice-cream cone.

He pauses to sip some tea, which are good for summarizing thoughts. He is quiet and I know what that means.

I can forget about a family outing to the Chiang Kai-shek memorial, and I suspect he hates our idea of circumnavigating the island. What a selfish idea that only an American banana could come up with.

Finally Dad breaks the silence, "Jaaames..., are you trying to get yourself killed?"

"I don't know," I say, "am I?"

"Zhaaat," Dad replies. It is a sound that only Asians make when frustrated by pressing the tongue on the roof of the mouth and then releasing the tongue.

"People do not drive to any set rules here," he says, "it's hazardous! I don't dare drive," he emphasizes by pointing to himself again with the cupped hands while shifting his leg from one over to the other.

He pauses again to sip some tea.

"Maybe I should go too," he says wagging his head. "Look, I will go with you" he says. "Much, much safer."

Much safer I think while sipping some tea. I'm starting to get that nauseous feeling again.

"Let's see," I reply, "let's see."

He sips some tea. Maybe we will spend our whole vacation sipping tea and avoiding friction. We are doing a lot better getting drunk on tea than avoiding friction. We sit and say nothing for three minutes.

"Let's do something fun today?" he finally says.

Finally, something we can agree on. We fully embrace with outstretched arms the warm fresh air alive with the scent of a recent downpour. It is cut with the sound of a thousand scooters lurching, screeching, and honking as we hit the street. A few late starters are slurping down their morning noodles at a makeshift restaurant on the curb. Dad has some ideas about what we are going to do for the day but I insist that we must first change some dollars to Taiwanese NT. I know Dad will want to pay for everything out of ancient pride but I have a sneaking suspicion he cannot afford it. Actually, I am positive he is penniless because he has always been so.

The final time I asked Dad for money was in my third year in college. I asked him to loan me five hundred dollars to get through the quarter and to his credit he came through in flying colors. When I asked him if he had trouble coming up with the money he said "no, not really. As soon as Mr. Lee realized I would blackmail him he forked it over," he emphasized with a karate chop and a wink. I wonder which relative he was chopping today?

I never asked him for money again even though to him it was perfectly fine to call in your favors when the time came. It's the Chinese way to do things, like shamelessly self-serving gift giving and axial greasing to lubricate the wheels and build guanxi. Connection building and the calling in of favors are all perfectly normal to his Confucian minded circuitry. It is hard for me, my eyes buried in the pledge of allegiance and the constitution, to reconcile the two systems. Nevertheless the money saved me and I never paid it back so how much superior am I?

We walk several blocks weaving in and out of traffic, stepping on and off walkways that do not meet any remote interpretation of ADA building code requirements. Even a high jumper could break a leg by stepping off the two-foot tall curbs that are built to assorted heights. Some walkways are blocked full of shoppers bargaining outside a store spilled over onto the street so that a pedestrian can not even see the treacherous grade change until shoved off by the crowd. We skirt along the side of the road to avoid this mishap. The compressed air from a bus sends our hair flying with black smoke out of unregulated mufflers painting our face ochre as it rumbles away.

I raise a brow at Lynn. Lynn is no neophyte to the second or third world. We met during our service as Peace Corp volunteers in Nepal. She has traveled to all points of the globe from India to Africa, amazingly to me, without fear. We decide single file is best from here on out, eyes pealed for incoming motorcycles, cars, trucks, buses, scooters, bicycles, mini cabs, maxi cabs and all who might harbinger death.

We are busy dodging obstacles left and right like a tailback busting through a crowded line. Not a speck of sun hits the concrete, there are people everywhere. Suddenly the rush is over and we are there. Dad plays the smiling doorman and opens the bank doors and the dry rush of conditioned air follows behind it.

The bank is a buzz with tellers in uniformed black blazers scattering like mice. Dad talks with a young moon faced girl with a crisp white shirt inside her spotless, pressed green blazer. She is dressed as prim and proper as a girl on her way to Catholic school. The next thing we know we are whisked away downstairs to a private desk. It looks like we are getting the royal treatment and do not have to wait for a teller like the common peasants in line. The peasants stare at us suspiciously.

I am embarrassed at the attention we are getting and experiencing a flashback to childhood. Dad is putting on a big show. All we needed was to change a little money. If there is such a thing as the Asian version of machismo, Dad is master machismo.

I am thinking, I would just like to change some money, please. No special favors, no long conversation, no tea and crackers. I suppose I am an uncultured rude young man.

Dad is thinking something else. He continues to chat with the young man behind the seat. He sits back at a rakish angle reminding the young manager of his superior age and place in the world simply because he is old. He has one leg over the other, one arm on a rest, the other holding his glasses, which he bites the corner of.

To add emphasis to his words he waves his glasses around in grand Wu-shu like circles. I do not understand the words but I have heard this conversation before, what theater. This may be how things are done here but I will never be able to play this game to much effect. I'm just too terse, too abrupt.

After about twenty to thirty minutes, the young manager finally turns to us and says, "your father tells me you are visiting from the states. Are you enjoying your stay?"

"Uh..., yes," I reply sitting up from my slouch.

"Do you wish to exchange some dollars?"

"Yes, yes, yes sir" I say.

He punches a solar powered calculator and shows me the day's rate.

"Great," I say, "please do it."

Apparently, this is not how it is done because Dad is now waving his glasses around. His back is stiff as a roster.

He crows, "No good rate!, bo-la, im-shi." He rises to leave and grabs my arm to follow. I don't move. Maybe Dad is trying to barter, but in a bank?

Lynn and I are stunned. We do not want to go after such a wait and we are torn. What happened to all the pleasantries and a half-hour of chitchat? I thought the two were long lost cousins or at least college frat brothers. Lynn and I are embarrassed at the unrestrained show of emotion; Dad is holding nothing back.

This can't be how this is done; Lynn's blank stare speaks. I can only stare back frozen with shame.

"Were on vacation, James" Lynn says, "can't you calm him down?"

Awakened from my trance, I use leverage to push Dad back into his seat.

But, Dad pops back up like a jack in the box and peers with a scowl at the banker. I have no idea why he is so ticked off. I wonder if it's an act or if this young man spit on our ancestor's grave?

The young banker appears apologetic to have ignited the wrath of an old man and is inconsolably sorry. He is lying on his back with his paws up begging for forgiveness. Now he is puckering up to Dad's posterior as if his own father were scolding him. So, *this is how it is done?*

The "old world" master and servant mentality is still at work inside Dad's mind and this is how it has always been done for him. After all these years I still cannot stomach it.

Dad is the center of attention. Every pause, every gesture is an opera. An eternal few seconds later, he says "so, it's okay with you Lynn?" as if handing down a pardon to the banker.

The banker face contorted in pain screams please, please let it be okay, Lynn.

"Yes!" Lynn says, "of course."

Nothing has ever been easy with Dad. His methods of approaching problems and solutions is literally foreign and anathema to me. They are completely illogical to me yet they make perfect sense to him. We are plainly wired as differently as an A.C. current is to a D.C. line without the benefit of an inverter. He is like an Apple computer and I am an IBM. There is yet no interface between the two.

The warm air outside is a relief. I am glad to have that business behind as we hail a taxi to Taipei proper. I am thinking *there is no way we are going to circumnavigate this island with Mr. Confucian Machismo* and spend the entire vacation stepping on eggshells.

The scenery flashes by in convulsive bursts of a strobe light. The taxi driver's foot is either completely on the gas or on the brake. The red tasseled Buddhist prayer ornament dangling from the rear view mirror flaps wildly as we bowl our way through traffic. When I was last in Taipei in the 1970's the taxis were little putt-putt Datsun tinfoil boxes, but now the taxis were fully grown Ford's, and Toyota's with horsepower to maim and kill. We fly across town weaving in and out of spaces seemingly impossible to fit a vehicle with an all too familiar random Asian style. We make so many turns through what look like alleys and private driveways that no traffic engineer could have planned. We make so many turns it seems we are drawing a circle.

The vectors we travel leaves an Euclidean trained geometrist like myself befuddled. I would like to believe this guy is trying to show off but he is driving just like everyone else is. As we step out of the car Lynn says "that guy is an asshole." My knuckles are white.

I nod, but we soon realize that he is just an average driver in Taipei. The notorious Asian driver found from India to Japan is a firm believer in "fate" and "face." These are two ancient ideas, which are incompatible with the invention of modern vehicular traffic signaling. The Taiwanese pilot will not think twice about taking incredible vehicular chances and will not back down easily from the slightest challenge from other drivers. It is a lovely combination in which the horn is used every five seconds to tell others "get out of the way low-po-aa (old lady) here I come!"

I doubt a deaf person could drive in most Asian cities without endangering themselves or others. If I were deaf I would not walk the streets of Taipei without a set of rearview mirrors permanently mounted on my head like a set of antlers, and reflectors on my back the size of coconuts.

Uncle's house is in community of one-eighth inch bulletproof steel gated homes shut tight as a drum. Some homes have gates that are camouflaged to look like architectural ornaments with flowery designs pressed into the steel. Others are simple ten-foot slabs of steel with not even a peephole to shed light through. However they are designed, the sheer quantity of steel is a sure sign of Taiwanese NT currency. Upscale neighborhoods like Uncle's near Tienmu is a virtual stockpile of the raw iron ore. An area such as this was a natural harbor for the large number of American expatriates that inhabited Taipei before American forces pulled out to normalize relation with the big red China.

Even in an upscale neighborhood like Tienmu, the streets are mere alleys and there is the striking absence of landscaping that softens American suburbs. There is concrete and more concrete and more concrete. Landscaping would require terra firma that could be used for a bedroom for grandma. As secure as the steel gated community appears on the surface, this would be the neighborhood to commit larceny. A gate is only a gate. Just ask the builder of the Great Wall of China. I picture master thieves mapping out every inch of this treasure trove.

Inside Uncle's gate is a small yard with a lone banana tree dwarfed by an elephantine concrete home sprouting skyward. The lot is no more than a postage stamp. One thousand five hundred square feet at the most. The obvious solution is up. Four stories with a penthouse the home reaches for un-shaded light. The roof offers the only unobstructed view of the mountains to the north.

We are introduced to my uncle on my father's side who I have never met or heard of. He is gracious and obviously a man of means. His house has all the amenities of a consumption loving suburban home in Beaverton, Oregon. He even has a karaoke machine connected to his big screen TV that he invites us to use during a party he insists to throw in our honor. My reaction is Puritanical, prudish, and typically American. A karaoke machine for gods sakes, what dorks. When it comes to our refined state pop culture I'm a snob. I look down on my Uncle's attempts at being cool but I'm sorry for not accepting later.

By comparison to all the rules and regulations built into my personality, Uncle is simple. If guests come they must be entertained. But, I'm too cool for *Pink Lady*. My uncle and his family are warm and unapologetically open up their home and hearts to us. For honored guests, hospitality is a tradition dating back to ancient times.

"When friends visit from afar, is this not indeed a pleasure?" wrote Confucius over 2,000 years ago. Taiwanese call this "the flavor of human feeling," ren-ching-wei which my uncle and family embody.[6]

A leather lined, fully down stuffed couch support our backs and we are bathed in luxury and a light conversation. Dad grows more at home by the second. He sinks back further and further until he is striking his reclining Buddha pose. With a cigarette in one hand, he makes magnanimous grand gestures drawing large trails of smoke in the air as he speaks. It is Chinese alpha male bonding body language. Although perfectly acceptable behavior to my Uncle, it makes the back of my neck hot.

"Aaha, haa, haa!," he laughs so very, very loudly at his own jokes. It is like a thousand little bamboo spears shot straight into my eyes. I am my father's harshest critic. My palms and feet are sweating just like they did a day ago at the arrival gate.

Thankfully, the conversation turns to Uncle. He has the floor and we learn that he is a self-made man who made his fortune importing electronic goods to Taiwan from Japan in the 1960's, 1970's and 1980's. That's a twist, importing electronic goods to Taiwan? The conversation turns again.

Dad and Uncle are thick as thieves chattering back and forth in Taiwanese. They are laughing and carrying on to the point of falling over each other. We stare at our feet and smile at Uncle's wife who does not ever say a word. She is meant to obey not to animate.

Several minutes pass, an eternity to be silent while two hyenas are braying.

Uncle finally turns to me to ask, "why do you want to visit the Chiang Kai-shek memorial?"

Here we go again, I think.

"He was a butcher of many Taiwanese," he adds with a deadpan look.

It didn't say anywhere in the travel book that Chiang Kai-shek was a butcher of Taiwanese people? I thought Chiang Kai-shek was Taiwanese?

"I...., I...., I...don't know," is all I can get out of my mouth.

Lynn comes to my rescue. She says, "what little I know about General Chiang is that he is the father of modern Taiwan. Did he not stand alone against the Communists after World War II? The travel book says he is credited with industrializing the island, and has always been an ally to America. He is a champion of Democracy and a converted Christian. Is that incorrect Mr. Yu?"

"Yeh…" I say.

"Aiiya James," uncle sighs, "don't you know anything about the history of your family? Your own history is the history of Taiwan itself."

The Pirate of Formosa

Confucius said:

"Coming from those in power, a system may be lacking in historical authority ("historical evidences"), however excellent it may be; what is lacking in historical authority cannot command credence; and what cannot command credence the people will never obey. Coming from those not in authority, a system may not command respect, however excellent it may be; what does not command respect cannot command credence; and what cannot command credence the people will never obey.

Therefore, every system of moral laws must be based upon the man's own consciousness, verified by the common experience of mankind, tested by due sanction of historical experience and found without error, applied to the operations and processes of nature in the physical universe and found to be without contradiction, laid before the gods without question or fear, and able to wait a hundred generations and have it confirmed without a doubt by a Sage of posterity...[7]*"*

On the day my life nearly ended at the hand of an ancient Nepali, Newar perched on the eyebrow of a cliff in the foothills of the Himalya, I realized nationality is an illusive definition not just for myself but for most Asians. When Mom and Dad were born on Taiwan, they were officially Japanese. Yet ethnically, Mom and Dad were descended from Ming and Fukienese immigrants from the south coast of present day China. Their families had been living in Taiwan for hundreds of years prior to Japan acquiring Taiwan as its first colony but they had never actually been back to China. *That is to say they did not necessarily think of themselves as Chinese any more than they thought of themselves as Japanese. This will make more sense in subsequent chapters.*

By the time they were in college, Japan had lost World War II and the allied command handed Taiwan over to the Nationalist Chinese forces under Chiang Kai-shek. By the time my parents had children they were Americans, and by the time their children were grown Mom was a baglady and Dad returned to Taiwan penniless and broken.

Through the course of their lives they had to learn first to speak Taiwanese, then Japanese, then Mandarin Chinese, then Latin, then English to cope with the changing landscape. Mom and Dad also learned Spanish, Italian and German in their wanderings. It is hard to say which is their native tongue. In light of their traumatic history, their nationality is not easily defined. While outside forces have always decided ownership of Taiwan to further one goal or another, none has ever bothered to ask my parents or any Taiwanese before what they themselves wanted. Sovereignty has always been dictated at the point of a sword or bayonet and may yet hold true to form with the communist threats.

The slippery slope of sovereignty and nationhood to our family are as sinuous and undefined as the growing embankments of the Himalya. In Peace Corps Nepal, I discovered the old man I met by the cliff was from a village of Newars perched up the trail. Chetries inhabited the village on the other side of the valley. Brahmins ran the teahouse at the bus stop in Ghorka. Sherpas and Gurungs lived further up the trail. Numerous other ethnic groups inhabit the small landlocked country of Nepal each with their own language, heredity, custom, food, and culture. Each is physically distinctive as well.

On the roof of Nepal, North of Mount Everest and the Himalya lies the expansive Tibetan plateau and there are more diverse groups of ethnic tribes inhabiting this region of current day China. If there is such amazing diversity in a peanut shaped, landlocked Asian country like Nepal, the size of Connecticut, then it is not hard to imagine what an immense landscape such as China has in store. Today, China's vast territory stretches from the cold dry northern plains all the way to the tropical shores of the South China Sea. From east to west it stretches from the impenetrable mountains bordering Pakistan all the way to the Korean Peninsula. Having to adapt to such a variety of climate and terrain as well as the pure physical distances would naturally create cultural pluralism and ethnic diversity. China is hardly the homogeneous society that many in the west perceive. On the surface Chinese culture, through its thousands and thousands of years of unabated assimilation has done much to mollify the distinctions between the peoples of north, south, east and west Asia. This is especially evident when it comes to language. But even the length and breath of Han Chinese culture, derived from the north, has not erased the memory of the distinctly separate origins of Southern Chinese people. When talking with a Southern Chinese person about people from Beijing they will often refer to them as "Northern peoples." Then, what about Taiwan?

The Yu and Yeh story on Taiwan begins approximately in the 16th century during which events around the world ushered in a new era, an era of tall ships from Europe beginning the Era of Exploration. It was the beginning of the end for Imperial China. The events altering China greatly affected my family and the history of Taiwan.

Jan Huygen Van Linschoten stood in the crow's nest of a Portuguese war ship bobbing like a cast iron tub in the turbulent Pacific. The Dutch navigator scanned the horizon for hints of the cutter's position in the cobalt marble sea. The year was 1590 and the warm South Pacific sun and air bleached his normally alabaster skin red and taught. His ship raced with the wind to the aft and cut like a knife through a deep blue crystal. Through his glass he spied to the west the green peaks of a tropical island, which grew on the horizon to the starboard side. *"Ilha Formosa, Ilha Formosa!!"* The navigator hailed to the crew.

Formosa means beautiful in Portuguese. My parents are from Beautiful Island. The Portuguese called the inhabitants Formosans, the beautiful people. Dark brown skinned and jet-black lacquered haired natives who lived close to the land. Some tribes grew millet to brew spirits, some grew taro for sustenance, some practiced the art of tattoo, and some ritual head hunted and cannibalized. At this time, the island was sparsely populated with a small constituency of immigrants from the Chinese continent living on the island. In 1500, Formosa's aborigines constitute 98% of the population, and Taiwan resembled nothing of the Republic of China it is called today.[8] The island was an undeveloped wilderness inhabited by mostly aborigines and a sprinkling of Chinese ethnic minorities in search of a better life. They were called Formosans by the west.

Almost four hundred years later, I was born on November 5th, 1966 in the Women's Hospital, the old wing of St. Luke's Hospital in Manhattan, New York. My birth certificate read, *to Father Poppet Jui-Chang Yu and Mother Charlene Chao-Ying Yeh of Formosa.* Born at 5:33 am, I was their third Formosan American child. I was born a Formosan American, a race constantly in transition, a race possibly earmarked for extinction.

The world around us today is a resounding reminder that the coming of the west drastically altered the course of history in Asia including Taiwan. In 1521 the Spanish explorer Ferdinand Magellan ended his attempt to circumnavigate the earth by expiring in the Philippines. One out of his five ships completed the journey and as a result, the Spaniards would return to colonize the Philippines.

The Portuguese colonized the south China port of Macau adjacent to Hong Kong in 1557. The Dutch fortified their position in Indonesia in 1619 and in 1624 fought China's Ming Dynasty for control over Penghu Island just west of Taiwan. The Dutch proceeded to occupy and control southwest Taiwan until Mom's relative Kuo Hsing-yeh drove them off thirty-eight years later.

How the relations on my mother's side of the family rose to historical prominence is indelibly tied to the events that lead to the end of the Ming Dynasty in 1644. Up until this time, Mom's progenitor and father of Kuo Hsing-yeh, Cheng Chih-lung was merely a Taiwan based pirate raiding the procession of trading ships stocked full of riches and spice that plied the waters around the island. Cheng Chih-lung interacted with pirate groups from Japan and Korea combining to torment the Ming Dynasty, which reigned for 276 years under 16 emperors from 1368 to 1644.[9] The pirates formed large armed gangs resembling a rogue navy.

Cheng Chih-lung eventually came to lead a gang of pirates, mercenaries, and traders based in Hirato, Japan where he married a Japanese wife, Tagawa.[10] Tagawa bore him a son Cheng Chen-kung (aka, Kuo Hsing-yeh). The pirates used Taiwan as a strategic point to intercept their prey. The location of the island was a natural post.

Within the context of the times in which Cheng Chih-lung and his son Cheng Chen-kung lived was an institutionalized policy of isolationism in China. Even at this early date, distrust of foreign, culturally polluting influences were abhorred by the Ming regime in power. Cultural isolationism by the Ming Chinese was to prove to be a lasting legacy and has only recently begun to show signs of abatement as western commercialization penetrates China. Initially it appears odd that the mechanisms for this conservatism would be in place so long before westerners invaded Beijing.

However, the Han Chinese majority has always lived under the specter of invasion from northern barbarians. The Ming hatred of foreigners was a consequence of Mongol dominance over the majority Han Chinese under the Yuan dynasty. The Ming Dynasty beginning in 1368 ensued by toppling the Mongol Empire consolidated by Chinggis Khan. The Mongols conquered China and governed the largest empire in the history of the world from 1279 to 1368 under the name Yuan. For the majority Han Chinese, the

Mongolian foreign language and customs were humiliatingly thrown onto the subdued majority and institutionalized in the royal court. Having a foreign power governing China left a wound in the psyche of the majority Han Chinese that never healed. When the majority Chinese finally wrestled power back from the northern barbarians under the flag of the Ming it was with the hope that such humiliation would never be repeated. The result of these experiences was a deep distrust of foreign forces and an inward looking society closed off from the modern revolutions that were affecting the outside world. The Ming were preoccupied with preserving the traditional Chinese culture and state. Furthermore, they were confronted with a perpetually armed border to the north where the horse-mounted tribes of archers lived and were always a threat.

Ironically, just short of three hundred years later the Ming succumbed to their greatest fear, invasion from the northern barbarians. This time, the Manchu bannermen from the north were knocking on the gates of the Great Wall of China. The wall itself illustrates the Han Chinese hysteria of trying to keep out invading northern foreigners as well as spy planes.

In another twist, the last Ming emperor Sze Tsung on the eve of his impending decapitation called upon Cheng Chi-lung to command the remnants of the Ming forces along with his pirate army in resisting the Manchu horde. Perhaps Cheng Chi-lung was a gambler or obscured with visions of Ming loyalties, after presumably years of raiding Ming vessels this seems strange, but Cheng answered the call to arms. By this time the fight was all but lost as Ming traitors simply opened the gates of the Great Wall and allowed the Manchus to overrun Beijing.

In its efforts to maintain social order, the Ming starting with its first Emperor Hongwu, chose the path of *wu* (violence) over *wen* (civil justice) in its philosophy of administering government. Choosing force (*wu)* over the civil (*wen)* path had over time alienated many in the Ming ranks. Along with the inevitable corruption and bureaucratic fat that accompanied almost every Imperial Chinese society, it was not surprising that Ming traitors had aided in the demise of the dynasty.[11]

China was yet again ruled by a foreign society as the Manchus took control of the royal court in 1644. The Manchus realized as a physical minority that they would need cooperation from the subdued Ming society to rule. As a result, they wisely combined force and enticement to undermine any potential opposition. High officials fleeing to the south were wooed back to the Manchu court proclaimed Ching ("Pure") dynasty.

Cheng Chih-lung on the loose with his army intact still posed a serious threat to the Ching. As a result, the Ching lured Cheng Chih-lung to Beijing with promises of court appointments and rank provided he swore allegiance to the new regime. Although the offer was viewed with suspicion, Cheng Chih-lung, always the gambler, decided to take the bait and along with his wife traveled voluntarily to Beijing.

The pirate commander was immediately betrayed, placed under house arrest when he refused to reveal the location of his forces, and his wife Tagawa defiled. Shortly after, Tagawa committed suicide.

When Cheng Chih-lung's half-Japanese son Cheng Chen-kung learned of his mother and father's fate, he abandoned his studies, grasped his sword and wagged his fist at the heavens swearing to avenge their wrong. Nothing would console the youth outside the blood of Manchu officials. He inherited his father's pirate kingdom and immediately became a scourge to the coastal cities of the south and east. Along with his father's enterprises, the son inherited the weighty Ming banner and with this new responsibility came the new name and title Kuo Hsing-yeh ("Lord of the Imperial Surname").

Kuo Hsing-yeh set himself about the work of attacking the Manchus to restore the Ming and his refusal to join his father in a Beijing prison ended in Cheng Chi-lung's execution in 1661. By 1660, fearing invasion and possible local support for Kuo Hsing-yeh, the Ching ordered all denizens of China's east coastal region to move inland 1.728 kilometers. The strategy was to starve out any local support for pirates and Ming loyalists who sought to re-supply at these locations and it worked. It also perpetuated the Ming isolationism, which the Ching[12] inherited in their attempts to retain power as a minority regime.

From his bases surrounding the straits of Taiwan, Kuo Hsing-yeh plotted his campaign to regain the motherland. With an army of 100,000 men and an armada of 3,000 war junks, he pressed on against the Manchus from 1646 until 1658. At his zenith, he nearly recaptured the capital of Nanking, but the Manchus ultimately pushed the Ming back into the sea by taking away any coastal bases from where they could launch interior campaigns. On advice from Ho-Bin, a translator for the Dutch East India Company, Kuo Hsing-yeh finally retreated back to the island bastion of Formosa which his father had used as a pirate base so many years before. The motherland was lost to the Ming forever by 1661.

By 1661 the Dutch had substantial control of the southern portion of Formosa and were well on their way to colonizing the entire island. Initially, the Dutch regarded Kuo Hsing-yeh as just another pirate of the sort they had seen for decades along the coast. They allowed Kuo Hsing-yeh to set up camp in northern Taiwan and to even smuggle large numbers of Ming loyalists to Formosa to man his armies and settle. By the time Kuo Hsing-yeh attacked the Dutch strongholds in the south in 1661, the Dutch were well aware of his name, which they called Koxinga. Koxinga may have been their best attempt at pronouncing the pirate's name.

The Dutch had grossly underestimated Koxinga. Shortly after, Koxinga drove the Dutch settlers to the safety of several coastal forts in the south and summarily lay siege to them all with 30,000 warriors. The Dutch were grossly outnumbered with just 2,000 soldiers and cut off although they undoubtedly had superior technology. After two years, the Dutch surrendered at Fort Zeelandia, outside of modern day Tainan. The Dutch governor and his surviving men were permitted to leave the island with their remaining possessions. The Dutch never came back and their rule over the southern portion of the island ended a mere 38 years after it began. With the end of Dutch rule came the end of the age of Ilha Formosa of Jan Huygen Van Linschoten as Chinese cultural influences would accelerate on the island from this time forward.

To summarize how events in 14th to 16th century China influenced the evolution of the Island of Taiwan it is important to understand the internal political climate of the Ming rulers and how they influenced Cheng Chih-lung and his son Koxinga. Up until the period of the coming of the western explorers, Taiwan was "outside the pale of Chinese civilization," as is recorded in the court records of the Han Chinese.[13] Chinese court chronicles of the Ming explorer Cheng Ho described Taiwan as a base for pirates, and did not record any evidence of a Chinese population on the island.[14] The Ming sent no further expeditions, as they were an Inland Empire concerned solely with preserving the seat of power of the traditional Chinese. Entrenched in their isolationism with the nightmare memories of the rule of Chinggis Khan and chronically concerned about invasion from the northern frontier, their interest in a frontier island teeming with non-Chinese aborigines and pirates seems unlikely.

However, the coming of the west and the invasion of the Ming from the north by the Manchus changed the history of Taiwan drastically. The Dutch controlled the southern portion of the island at present day Tainan where they erected Fort Zeelandia and hung their sovereign flag. The demise of the Ming drew our pirate relatives into the struggle and would eventually lead to the liberation of Formosa from the Dutch colonizers.

The Pirate Who Would Be King

Mom's family arrived on Taiwan with Koxinga in 1661 and has never set foot on Mainland China. My father's family arrived on the island around the same time from Fukien province. Seeking a better life, they have also never returned to the mainland. In light of these facts it is not surprising that they speak of a feeling of separateness from the power brokers in Beijing, a separateness they call Taiwanese.

To begin with, Mom's progenitor was half Japanese and was avowed to overthrowing the illegitimate Manchu regime in China that had raped and killed his mother and executed his father through deception. Those were hardly conditions that would draw flag waving loyalty to the Ching dynasty regime from the pirate king. Ironically, Chinese scholars have expressed the opinion that Koxinga, with the expulsion of the Dutch, owns the title of the first Chinese king of Taiwan. Which Chinese are they talking about Manchu or Ming or are they speaking of a cultural link, or are they speaking of a genetic link? The claim is both true and false and is an oversimplification of a complicated history.

Mom always said, "you are Taiwanese," and this is what she meant. You come from Koxinga, the first non-European or Aborigine ruler of Taiwan, who was both Chinese and Japanese. You come from relatives who regard Taiwan as their permanent home and have ever since 1661 knowing virtually nothing about anything else. There is little doubt that they are derived from what today would be considered ethnic Chinese but further separation and ties have eroded those links, as we shall see. Their situation parallels Americans of English, German or Polish heritage. Few would still consider themselves English, or otherwise, as many have mixed ancestry and may have never themselves traveled to their country of origin.

Having sworn allegiance to the Ming, it is not surprising that Koxinga constructed an administrative government in its image. The Ming entourage that accompanied him across the straits was composed of over 1,000 scholars, artists, monks and masters of every branch of the Ming's very popular culture at the time. Koxinga ushered in a renaissance of many ancient Chinese laws, institutions, customs, song and dance. It made for the strange situation that is paralleled today with the communists of Taiwan actually adopting traits culturally more traditionally Chinese than their respective counterparts in Beijing. On top of his cultural achievements, he developed Taiwan's infrastructure by creating a transportation network of roads. Proper roads could rapidly transport the growing amount of surplus crops that were harvested as a result of strides in agricultural technology and the simple fact that more land was put under the plow. Acting on the Chinese timeless valuation of education, he instituted a school system that could feed the new nation's needs for an educated labor force.

Quite naturally, Fort Zeelandia became the first capital of the island where the government court was established. The City of Tainan grew around the fort and evolved into the island's first capital city. The location and industry of the people catapulted Tainan into the political and commercial center of the island. Anping, close by, grew into a booming harbor town. Taiwan experienced the first economic surge of the kind that would come and go with the tides of each new regime in the future.

Today, the accomplishments of Koxinga are highly revered on both sides of the Taiwan Straits, not bad for the son of a pirate. The pirate had become a king. Koxinga is honored as *chun tzu*, a perfect man in the eyes of adoring Chinese scholars.[15] Mom's progenitor is deified in China and Taiwan and revered like Joan of Arc to the French. Along with rule came millions of ping of land passed on to his family. Ironically, Koxinga's rule over the island only lasted one year after conquering Taiwan. Koxinga died unexpectedly in 1683 at the prime age of thirty-eight.

Without the vision of Koxinga and riddled with court intrigue, his son and grandson were only able to retain rule over the island until 1684 when the Manchus finally succeeded in imposing quasi sovereignty over the island. Snuffing out the last pockets of Ming patriotism was not quite as simple and may never have occurred. There were so many clashes between the local population and Manchu officials that the island was described as "every three years an uprising, every five years a rebellion."[16]

Regardless of the ruler's loyalties or motivations, the arrival of Koxinga did mark the beginnings of a significant Chinese presence on the island. Large numbers of Ming loyalists fled to the island at this time and the island experienced a population explosion of the kind it would see more of in the future. However, the majority of the island was still under the control of the majority population of Aborigines so it cannot be stated that Koxinga had administrative control over the entire population. Nor did the Manchu rule that suppressed the Koxinga regime have full authority of Taiwan. To be a Ching official exiled to the frontier of Taiwan was an unenviable position and the Manchu rule in Taiwan was plagued with corruption, graft and outright apathy. The Manchus only made claims to the western side of the island where the tablelands of the island could support agriculture. The eastern portion of the island remained an aboriginal frontier of old.

The Issue of Sovereignty

In the days leading up to and before the age of Koxinga sovereignty was as simple as having men and arms capable of subduing weaker, less sophisticated societies of primitive peoples. This was especially true in sparsely populated areas of the world but today this would serve as a poor recipe for nation building even as it is wantonly employed. Even in the age of Confucius, the issue of legitimacy or a mandate to rule from heaven was a rational criterion that the ancient sage espoused as fundamental for a government to survive. This is what he meant when he said, "People must have sufficient to eat; there must be a sufficient army; and there must be confidence of the people in the ruler."[17] When asked which two he would give up and still maintain a government, Confucius replied "There have always been deaths in every generation since man lived, but a nation cannot exist without confidence in its ruler."[18] Taiwanese, from the very day Koxinga set foot on the island, have been at odds with the Mainland authorities in Beijing starting with the Manchus who murdered the parents of the first Taiwanese national hero. Taiwanese have inherent legitimacy issues concerning Mainland claims of sovereignty over the island starting from the beginning and growing ever wider ever since. This is what my Uncle and father were trying to tell me when they asked "why do want to visit the Chiang Kai-shek memorial?"

It should be apparent by now that the issue of sovereignty over Taiwan is complicated indeed. To examine the issue further requires first a definition of the concept of sovereignty itself. A single definition of the word is inadequate as the formation of nations appears relative to the times during which they evolved. In the past, war, colonialism, and de facto might makes right was a popular method of nation building as in the case of our home America. Historic possession, ethnic background, de jure agreements have made for fine arguments as well. Each has been used in the rationalization of ruling parties in Taiwan.

In more recent history, the ideas of democracy or self-determination have become a popular ideological basis for nationhood. As involuntary and instinctive are the concepts of democracy to Americans, the ideology shares only a minor blip in the timeline of history. It is interesting to note that Taiwan has never actually experienced the use of this rationalization to form the basis of rule over the island until the transfer of executive authority that occurred in the 1996 elections. In fact, Taiwan is the first Asian nation to have metamorphosed into a consensus styled democracy since the beginning of recorded history and has only achieved the distinction within the past few years. It is a considerable feat. Still, Taiwan remains to be recognized as a nation by the international community.

Under traditional international law adopted by the United Nations, nationhood is defined by four qualifications: territory, population, government, and diplomatic ties.[19] Given these criteria, it is hard to imagine the current state of Taiwan as anything but sovereign. However, in a world where the communist government in Beijing possesses veto power in the Security Council of the U.N., it is otherwise. The Mainland government currently considers Taiwan to be a "renegade province" and has made it clear its intentions to recover the territory by any and all means; perhaps hinting to the old might makes right formula of securing national borders. Beijing has forwarded the argument that Taiwan has always been a part of China and has put forth several examples of ancient Chinese connections to the island as evidence.

Beijing invokes the theory of historical possession and ethnic ownership as the basis of their claims. To examine these claims it is necessary to go back even further in time, to a time more distal than the age of exploration and beyond the days of Koxinga. It is necessary to travel into Neolithic China when Taiwan was an Aboriginal Nation.

Twelve thousand years before the birth of Christ, warm marshes, lakes and wetlands characterized the plains that now exist between current day Shanxi and Shandong province. The warm moist climate of Paleolithic China had not yet cooled to the arid and colder temperatures today. The plains between the east and west mountain chains that are cultivated today did not exist in the warmth of primordial China. Shan (mountain) and xi (west) means "west of the mountains and Shandong means "east of the mountains. Provinces in China are commonly named for their position relative to natural features.

Neolithic Chinese society, beginning approximately 12,000 B.C., emerged quite rationally along the southern bend of the Yellow River at the meeting place of uncultivable wetlands and densely forested uplands. These grasslands were the place that could support a settled agricultural population. Water was not far away and the forest was a natural grocery for meat.

To understand the relationship of the emergence of Neolithic Chinese society and the ancient origins of Taiwan it is necessary first to come to grips with the sheer geographic immensity of the Chinese continent.

As we travel west from the delta of the Yellow River, which empties into the Yellow Sea boarding the Korean Peninsula, inland to its source in the mountains our journey begins. The river divides China north and south along approximately the 36 parallel at its delta. Beijing is perched a few degrees north at approximately 40-degree north latitude midway between Portland, Oregon and San Francisco, California. The Yellow River forms the boundary between Hebei

Province to the north, where Beijing is centrally located, and Shandong Province to the south. Hebei literally means "north of the river." It is at approximately the intersection of the southern tip of Hebei Province and the northern tip of Shandong Province where Neolithic society began along the river.

By contrast, Hong Kong on the South China Sea is at the 20th parallel near Cuba and Taiwan's most northern cities are situated at approximately Key West, Florida about 24 degrees north latitude. Taiwan is separated further by ocean from China.

Had we the ability to travel back in time to Neolithic China and retraced a journey along the Yellow River from its delta in the east our modern maps would have been useless. Where we would have expected to see endless fields of green pastures characterizing the great North China Plain today resembling the American Midwest, there would be water. There would be water as far as the eye could see. The Yellow and Yangzi Rivers had not yet deposited the sediments that built the plains between Shanxi and Shandong Province. Shandong Province floated as virtually an island off the coast. The Provinces of Hubei and Hunan located at approximately 30 degrees north latitude were uninhabitable swamplands unable even to support the cultivation of rice.[20] These uninhabitable areas were still over a thousand miles away from the south coast of China. With the cooling of the climate and the scouring power of the rivers, the formation of geography we see today evolved over thousands of years.

As a result, the early Neolithic societies of the Three Dynasties, Xia, Shang, and Zhou developed as a landlocked sedentary agricultural society. They were landlocked in a sense even greater than the geography of current day China would suggest. Tribes settled from the north bore no resemblance to the seafaring societies of the south, which were genetically and culturally distinct from the north. Over time the more culturally powerful and politically organized Northerners would eventually filter south and dilute Southern distinctions. Neolithic culture along the South China coast and Taiwan are more akin to those of the societies inhabiting Southeast Asia and Austronesia.

The obvious reason why there is little if no evidence to support Neolithic Chinese claims to Taiwan is because there were no Chinese living in the areas that were accessible points of immigration to the island at the time.[21] This statement should be refined to remind the reader that a distinction is being made between Northern and Southern Chinese peoples that does not exist today because of the assimilation of Southern peoples today by Han Chinese culture and political boundaries. But at the time, China was indeed "beyond the pale" of Chinese civilization. It was not until the Ming dynasty (1368-1644) that its precise location was determined. Prior to the Ming, China's ruler appeared confused in court records as to where the island was or what to call it.[22]

Consequently, more than ten thousand years of anthropologic history predates claims of Chinese Authority on Taiwan. Perhaps the oldest Chinese historical record referring to Taiwan indicates that the island was called the "land of Yangchow" before the rise of the Han dynasty in 206 B.C.[23] An attempt to explore the island may have been recorded in the *Shih Chi* during the Three Kingdoms period that followed. Compiled by Ssu-ma Ch'ien, it called Taiwan "Yichow."[24]

Beijing now quotes as evidence the legal basis of claim to Taiwan based on the precedence of discovery by referencing the Kingdom of Wu's exploration of the island in A.D. 239. According to the *San Kuo Chi*, the *History of the Three Kingdoms*, the emperor sent a 10,000-man expeditionary force to explore the island. However, there are no records of following missions, nor were any territorial claims proclaimed. Furthermore, the expedition resulted in the proclamation that the island was "outside the pale of Chinese civilization."[25]

In subsequent dynasties, as other leaders emerged in China, new emperors commissioned adventures to further explore Taiwan but the results were similar to previous investigations. This explains why by the relatively advanced year of 1500, 98% of the island was still inhabited by only aborigines.[26] It had been so for at least 15,000 years. The northern societies of Han Chinese never took to Taiwan as a home, their civilization developing in a landlocked agricultural belt as foreign to the island as a far away mosquito infested wilderness can be.

This also explains why by the time the famous Ming explorer Cheng Ho visited the island, he had proclaimed its "discovery" yet again even as others had previously come and gone beyond memory. Furthermore, he reports only of his encounters with the aborigine population reporting on their magical powers of healing. He does not mention any Chinese population living on the island. The name for the island as Taiwan was recorded in the Imperial registry for the first time meaning, "terraced bay." Another explanation why there was virtually no Chinese living on Taiwan by this time, even though the island was clearly visible from the mainland, is that it was illegal. The Ming fearing constant harassment from our pirate relatives, and an inward looking isolationist regime to begin with, mandated an imperial edict to ban emigration of the empire to Taiwan or anywhere else. Thus, any Chinese immigrants up until 1644 who ventured to seek a better life in Taiwan had done so illegally.

By the age of exploration when the Dutch landed in 1590, it is not surprising that they reported no signs of any administrative structure of the Chinese Imperial government. This explains how the Dutch were able to simply land their vessels and proclaim the island as a Dutch colony with no resistance from Beijing.

No one can say with complete accuracy when the first Chinese immigrants arrived on Taiwan because it was an illegal act and would by its nature prefer to remain a secret. What is clear is that even by 1661 when Koxinga expelled the Dutch there was only a sprinkling of ethnically Chinese population on the island. Among the earliest to arrive from the mainland were the Haaka and the Fukienese, the later of which my father is descended. Because there were no records, it is debatable as to which was first. Some even claim that Japanese migrants preceded the Haaka and Fukienese but there is little remaining evidence of this. What is known is that by the thirteenth century, Fukienese were already battling with and displacing Haaka from the choicest land.[27]

Ironically, the Haaka had earlier displaced the indigenous populations for the best farming land as well. Thus, the beginnings of ethnic struggle on Taiwan were born and continue to this day. Nor were the Hakkas considered Chinese themselves. Hakka literally means "stranger," or "guest." They were not welcome in Hunan Province by the majority Chinese and were relentlessly pursued, persecuted and driven to the safety of the offshore wilderness. Once on the island, they set about driving out other groups of natives who were weaker than them. Among the shared traits of all of the native peoples of Taiwan is the martial dominance by outside forces.

Many Fukienese share a similar feeling of separateness from the Han Chinese in Beijing as they are an ethnic minority in China today having developed far from the cradle of the Yellow River. Currently, Taiwan is inhabited by three major categories of ethnic groups within which there are many subsets. The three major categories are the 1) Aborigine who make up approximately 2% of the population, the 2) majority Taiwanese derived from Southern Chinese peoples, who have inhabited the island for hundreds of years, and the 3) Mainland Chinese, who immigrated with Chiang Kai-shek after losing China to the Communists after World War II.

Taiwanese comprised of Haaka, Fukienese, Ming, Japanese mixtures, etc constitute over 80 percent of the population, the Mainlanders who hail from all parts of China 10-15 percent and the Aborigines now make up only 2 percent of the population. The numbers are a drastic reversal from 1500 when 98 percent of the island was Aborigine and speaks to the traumatic events, which characterized the history of the island since the time of Koxinga. But who was the first Formosan's, who was the original man?

It may come as a surprise to many that the first Taiwanese were Polynesian, yet those appear to be the facts. Compared to the short four to five hundred years of recent history, which altered everything on the island and in the world, the ten to fifteen thousand years of potential inhabitation of the island, by Aborigines is an eternity. As discussed earlier, there was little likelihood of a Neolithic path of immigration from the Northern interior of China to Taiwan but the Polynesians have sailed the earth for time immemorial. Recent archeological digs along the banks of the Peinan River near Taitung place the original man in Taiwan as early as 10,000 years back. Not even the most optimistic proponent of Chinese historical claims of sovereignty over Taiwan can argue of earlier Chinese roots.[28]

Hunter-gatherer, subsistence farmer, and leathery seafaring people migrated to the island from various points of South and East Asia and are Taiwan's original denizen. There are officially nine tribes recognized by the Taiwanese government the Ami, Atayal, Bunun, Paiwan, Puyuma, Rukai, Saisyat, Tsao and Yami. Quite plainly, they are not Chinese names. The tribes exist till this day on the island as a small minority composing approximately 1.8 percent of the population just short of 23 million.[29] You can still meet a Taiwanese man or woman with curly hair or even an afro, like my Aunt has.

It is unlikely that all of the tribes came from the same place given the geographic accessibility of the island. There are various theories as to where each came from. Those with Polynesian connections have particularly strong evidence to suggest their origins, such as recent DNA testing.[30] As much as two-thirds of the words used by several of the tribes are the same in Malay and indicate ties to societies on the Malay Peninsula and Indonesian archipelago.[31] Archeologists have described the island as the northern most outpost of Polynesian culture.

Other theories abound such as conjecture as to the Aborigine connection to the Ryukyu Island people of Japan, or the Miao of the south coast of China. There are even some scholars who see Aboriginal ties with certain peoples inhabiting Mongolia. It may be that they are all of the above, but what they all share was an ethnic distinction from Han Chinese. Even the Miao who hailed from southern China speak a separate language, are culturally distinct and at the time of their arrival on the island had much less to do with a Han Chinese person from the Yellow River civilizations than a person from Thailand.

However, the Polynesian connection to Taiwanese Aborigines remains obvious as is evidenced by their bold tattoos and language. But who was the father and who was the son? Did the Polynesians or Austronesians originate in the South Pacific and colonize northward or did the peoples of the South Pacific originate on the Asian mainland and colonize southward. There are arguments on both sides. For the sake of our discussion it will suffice to say that anthropologists have many theories but what they seem to agree on is that the original man in Taiwan was non-Chinese.

To focus in on the fuzzy picture over the issue of sovereignty and China's claims of historical legal ownership of Taiwan, it may be helpful to revisit the timeline of the tropical temptress' complex history.

To begin, the first inhabitants of the island were Aborigine, (non-Chinese), and can be traced back as far as Neolithic China, when the idea of China itself was born. Anthropologists confirm that the Aborigine have lived on the island for 10,000 to 15,000 years. As the Chinese continent was vastly different geographically than it is today, the Han Chinese people were even more isolated from the people of the south.

Ethnically Chinese influences on the island are a relatively recent occurrence considering the long history of the island and blossomed with the arrival of Koxinga the first Taiwanese king. Although no one knows when the first Chinese immigrated to the island what is known is that by the thirteenth century small numbers of Haaka and Fukienese were already battling over the best farming land. However, it was with Koxinga that the island experienced a population explosion of Ming loyalists escaping persecution. From 1661 to 1684 the Koxinga regime administered control over mainly the southern portion of the island. By 1684, court intrigue and infighting between the right of ascension between Koxinga's sons led to the Manchu invasion. A new regime emerged under the Ching dynasty Bannerman administering control of Taiwan from afar. The Ching, heralding from Manchuria, had conquered China by 1644 and would retain control over the mainland until 1911. The Ching would rule Taiwan for the next 212 years during which Taiwan was within the fold of Beijing even though there was constant unrest.

Finally, even as historical claims of evidence that China owns the *legal* rights to Taiwan make for a weak argument, given the long history of the island, we need also examine more recent history starting from the year 1684. By 1684 Beijing did have control of at least the western portion of the island. Furthermore, a visit to Taiwan today would reveal that no other cultural influence to the island has been as significant as the Chinese. It appears that Chinese culture is the great assimilator of Asian peoples. However, this does not explain why every poll conducted of the Taiwanese express a longing for separateness and sovereignty.

It is an idea long suppressed in the mind of my uncle and father. From our observations of ancient Taiwanese history it is not hard to see why the indigenous peoples felt separate from outsiders. The birth of Taiwanese nationalism is not a recent phenomenon. However, on the surface it is less clear how the emergence of this Taiwanese-ness grew during the time of my father, his father, and in the age of the father of my grandfather.

The Emergence of Taiwanese Nationalism

If nothing else, it should be clear that Taiwan is a melting pot and always has been. It has always floated on the mist beyond the gaze of Beijing, a haven for pirates, castaways, Aborigines and outlaws. The first words that ever stuck in my infant brain could have been Taiwanese, Japanese, Mandarin Chinese, or English, a mixed vocabulary.

Yet western journalists and Washington seem to express a surprise at the *sudden emergence* of Taiwanese separatism as exposed in the now infamous German radio interview of Taiwan President Lee Teng-hui. Lee asserted that Taiwan should treat China on a "state-to-state," basis in 1999. Clearly indicating abandonment from the one-China formula of the Chiang Kai-sheks Nationalists he added, "under such special nation-to-nation relations, there is no longer any need to declare Taiwanese independence."[32]

An Article in the *New York Times* on July 14, 1999 began "What in the world is Taiwan's President up to?"[33] The article went on to express the universal puzzlement of China scholars and American Diplomats at the sudden shift of Mr. Lee and his claims of a Taiwanese separateness. Not surprisingly, China responded with the usual threats and expressions of resolve to reunite the motherland.

However incredulous some politicians may have appeared, I doubt the announcement could really have been so surprising to scholars who have bothered to look beyond the last forty years of Taiwanese history. The emergence of Taiwanese nationalism is older than the Bible. That Mr. Lee made the announcement as the first democratically elected and first Taiwanese born President of the island should also not be a surprise. Mr. Lee is an ethnic Haaka who were among one of the ethnic minorities in China to be persecuted and driven off the mainland. What should be surprising is that such an announcement has not been made earlier considering the makeup and will of the Taiwanese people. This statement is somewhat inaccurate as there have been several attempts by the Taiwanese to declare independence but each attempt was quickly suppressed. It is a testament to the level of suppression that the Chinese Nationalist regime exerted on the island for the past forty years and of those who have ruled before.

There is a very good reason why Mom and Dad speak fluent Japanese; it is because they were Japanese citizens when they were born. One might of expected that in 1683 when the Manchus took over Taiwan and established passive rule over the Western portion of the island that the issue of whether or not the inhabitants of Taiwan were Chinese or not would have been over. The opposite occurred.

The period of rule under the Ching dynasty is characterized as "Every three years an uprising, every five years a rebellion."[34] Between 1683 to 1843, there were fifteen major rebellions and over 100 recorded revolts against the Ching giving the island the dubious distinction as the "land of rebellion and unrest."[35]

The inhumane treatment of the Taiwanese, corrupt and apathetic Chinese officials, and the economic stagnation of the island is cited as proof to the Taiwanese that Beijing did not truly regard Taiwan to be a part of the empire. For court officials' banishment to the Taiwanese frontier was more punishment than a prized commission and once engaged they would count the days until it was over. It did not help that the Ching were actually foreigners to China derived from Manchuria and ironically feared the "Chineseness" of the people on

Taiwan. As a result, Taiwaneseness grew under Chinese rule instead of receding. Ties to the mainland grew weaker and weaker with each generation. Furthermore, the Ching fostered ambiguity over the sovereignty on the island when it was convenient to do so. The Ching had ordered over one hundred thousand Chinese to return to the mainland and isolated the island by restricting travel to it. Furthermore, they had previously ordered the Chinese coastal population inland which along with other regulations made Taiwan into a clearinghouse for illegal activity. Taiwan became a smuggler's paradise along with rampant illegal immigration, and piracy.

Taiwanese were determined to squeak out a better life for themselves in spite of the Ching rules. Taiwanese pirates continued to raid American, Japanese and French ships. When faced with formal complaints from the international powers over the treatment of their cargo, Beijing responded by stating, "Taiwan is beyond our territory," thus absolving themselves from any legal responsibility for the events.[36]

The malaise over the continued piracy lead to gunboat diplomacy by the French who sent a fleet into Keelung harbor. The French contingent landed and invaded Tamsui as well. For nine months in 1884-1885 northern Taiwan was declared French territory.[37]

Shortly after the French invasion the Ching government finally decided to declare Taiwan an official province of the empire calling it Taiwan Province. Embroiled with the Japanese in growing tensions, which eventually exploded into war in 1894 over Korean suzerainty, China would once again lose control of Taiwan-this time "in perpetuity." By losing the war with Japan over Korea, the Chinese ceded Taiwan and the Pescadores to Japan "in perpetuity," according to the Treaty of Shimonoseki. The international community recognized the treaty as legal and binding giving the Japanese a legitimate claim to Taiwan in the eyes of the world.[38]

For the Taiwanese, their nationality had changed overnight and to make matters worse, the Ching had not informed the population of the power transfer. Taiwanese only learned of the deal first from foreign traders. The Taiwanese were stunned and wondered how a war fought in northern China had resulted in their home being given away lock stock and barrel. A few community leaders banded together and saw the void in leadership as an opportunity to declare independence. Having little knowledge of how to govern they boldly established a new government named the Republic of Taiwan. It was Asia's first republic. For Taiwanese today, it is no coincidence that Taiwan has become, once again, the first transitional democracy in Asia. The longing of the people to set a course of their own has been long in the making.

Nevertheless, the Republic of Taiwan was in no position to fend off the highly mechanized Japanese war machine once they landed. Japan established Taiwan as its first colony in 1895 and did not relinquish control until the end of World War II in 1945 when it lost all its colonies. The Taiwanese people were once again thrown into a new era of rule under another outside force. It was a rule that lasted fifty years during which my father and mother were born.

My first visit to my mother's childhood home in Tainan, built on land bequeathed to Koxinga, could have just as easily been a trip to Kyoto, Japan. Straw tatami mats, moveable wood and rice paper sliding partitions, black lacquered finishes adorned my grandfather's house, an obvious legacy of the fifty years of Japanese rule. The fifty years of Japanese rule in Taiwan set the people even further adrift of the bonds of the mainland.

By now relatives on both sides of my family were far removed from a Mainland identity having never seen it except through the examples of the Manchus. What is more is the growth of the Japanese identity. Although it is undeniable that the Japanese treated Taiwan as a subdued colony, when compared to the corrupt and incompetent Ching, Taiwanese preferred the disciplined and rational rule of the Japanese. Unlike the Ching Chinese, the Japanese invested intensively in the island creating an economic and social boom. Law and order was restored, with a heavy hand at times, by ending the local warlordism.

Japan was the first government to finally gain control over the entire island, something Koxinga and the Ching could never do. Tokyo concentrated efforts at agricultural expansion of the island. With Taiwan's expansive western plains there was actually more cultivable land on Taiwan than in Japan. By the 1930's the colony produced twice as much rice as the people needed with nearly a million tons exported to the motherland Japan. Sugar was also exported as a surplus.

Japan also invested in the building up of Taiwan's infrastructure by adding ten times the amount of railroad to the island by 1905. Seven thousand more miles of railroad were planned for construction at this time.[39] Hydroelectric projects made Taiwan the first electrified region of Asia outside of Japan. The list goes on and on. It is no wonder that my father says, "life was more just under the Japanese."

His sentiments are shared by a great many his age. On my mother's side of the family the sentiments are the same and quite natural since Koxinga's mother Tagawa was Japanese to begin with. In other words, Mom is part Japanese and there was very little culturally to overcome with the transference of power. Their family prospered tremendously under the Japanese. My mother's brother Richard Yeh is married to a Japanese woman, as are many Taiwanese men. My father's sister is married to a Japanese man. There are blood ties older than the history of the United States.

Taiwanese even served as soldiers in the Japanese army in World War II, helping to invade Mainland China! There is little doubt that atrocities occurred in Taiwan under the Japanese as in other parts of Asia. But in comparison with previous regimes, many Taiwanese held the Japanese in regard. It was simply a matter of degree. However, by the end of World War II, Taiwan was on the wrong side of history.

Dad was shot in the ear by an American Mustang flying low over the rice paddy he crossed to get home from school. He was left for dead in a ditch next to the bicycle he was walking. Taiwan would be offered on the table once again by outsiders who cared nothing for, nor asked the opinion of the people living there. A perpetual pawn in another chess game, Taiwan was temporarily placed in the care of the

Nationalist Chinese under Chiang Kai-shek during the Cairo Conference in December 1943. However, no legal basis was established for the transfer of power to the Chiang regime. Faced with a life and death struggle with the communists on the Mainland, Chiang would eventually transfer his army and regime onto the island with the communist victory.

Although, the Ming never gave up hope of reunifying the mainland under its banner, it would have to stand in line today behind the Chinese Nationalists. The coming of Chiang Kai-shek strangely mirrored events 300 years earlier with the arrival of Koxinga. With the Nationalist beaten to Taiwan came a return to Chinese rule over Taiwan and the assertion that Taiwan was the real China. Even though 90% of the Taiwanese population had grown far away from the sphere of Chinese rule another government and the Mandarin Chinese language was thrown upon them. With Chiang came the one-China policy assertion that has always rang false to my father and mother. Forty years of martial law followed. Given the opportunity to travel and study abroad, Mom and Dad escaped Nationalist China they thought never to return.

Chiang Kai-shek Memorial

Oakland, California born author Amy Tan, has said that the moment her feet touched China, she became Chinese. Many other overseas Chinese have expressed the same fundamental connection to their legacies in China even as they were hatched from all points of the globe.[40] Perhaps, it is the specific gravity of such a massive history. They discover their time overseas appears no more than a speck on the timeline of their family tree.

A first time pilgrim to her homeland, Ms. Wong, a math teacher from San Francisco, California stated, "it's good just to be surrounded by people who look like you."[41] Others report the same inner sensation even for those who do not speak the language or know the customs. They come home feeling they have discovered something intrinsic within them that was always there and always would be, their Chinese-ness.

It must be for many their first taste of being part of a majority. The powerful feeling and the longing to fit into something bigger than a lonesome overseas immigrant may be what they share. It must be a wonderful feeling. It was the reason I returned to Taiwan to visit my father.

"Go then!" Dad said. So we went.

The cab emptied Lynn and I at the gapping mouth of the cyclopean quadrangle built to honor Generalissimo Chiang Kai-shek. We stood gazing as if on mountains of the cascading marble gates, stairs, and pillars, which framed the heavens. The sheer size of the monument lifted our gaze toward the stratus vespers growing with the winter moisture in the air.

It is the perfect setting for my Amy Tan moment. The moment that I had been hoping for and traveled so far to find. The last time I gazed at this patch of sky was in 1971. I recall the humming of Red Chinese bombers dusting low over their targets. It was a carnival for us to be frolicking outside so deep into the night but no one with a pulse was going to sleep tonight. The heavy air of a windless night matted my greasy hair.

We moved like pubescent bats through the stifling moonless night. Chiang Kai-shek has ordered every light in Taipei off and the darkness is palatable. In the primordial dark, the vibrations from the air defense sirens resonate through my whole body like a hammer striking a tuning fork. I'm not sure which is worse the nerve tingling sensation of the sirens or the complete silence of the fathomless night where only the restrained, nervous laughter from a passing flock of teenagers pass like a breeze. The young roam the streets tonight. If they are to die it will not be inside a concrete building collapsed around them.

My cousin's pocket is my lifeline as he feels his way through the tar, black streets. We pass a group huddled around the crackling of an AM transistor radio.

"Off!" Eldest cousin implores drawing a finger across his neck.

It is Halloween without candy or light and the promise of instant annihilation. It is my first taste of war and it leaves my underpants tainted. They dry hard and crusty scratching my legs as we walk downtown. Mom and Dad sent us into a war zone?

As the hours pass, we grow accustomed to the moan of the propeller driven bombers above until their haloed lighting stop us like deer caught in headlights. Pedestrian's scatter like mice as the line of glowing, spotlight moons run across the asphalt bathing them in light and stripping away their anonymity. It's useless to run and we stare up at them blindly, blinking; Americans caught in the crossfire.

The communist's did not drop their armaments on us that evening. I lived to wonder where General Chiang lay hidden during those hours as Lynn and I ran our fingers over his bust in the great hall of his memorial.

"He made a lot of enemies," Lynn said.

My father and my uncle spat on the floor when we invited them to give us a tour, one of their saliva-less spits. After my visit with my uncle and our talk with my Dad, it was clear that I was not going to have my Amy Tan moment at the memorial.

"If you want to visit a memorial to your ancestors then go to Tainan," Uncle said, "you can honor your ancestors at the Koxinga shrine."

Even as my relatives re-calibrated my compass to the south, I wished to understand why Chiang provoked such a response from the old men.

"You know er er ba was taboo," Dad said. "We never wanted the KMT to whisk you away to Green Island in the night," he added.

"During those times, how many mothers were crying overnight for their children imprisoned on Green Island" Uncle added.

"What are you talking about," I asked, "you sent us into a war zone?"

"Aiiya, James it is not kid business," Dad replied.

"It has been martial law, martial law from 1949 till 1987!" Uncle interjected.

"Dua-la!" Dad confirms.

Though the two men cannot simply come out and say it, I have seen Dad full of apprehension before but this is different. Even now, they are paralyzed beyond words much less action. I wanted my selfish closure but they were not forthcoming with information to give on this topic. They are reluctant historians, so I am resigned to explore my own research. It is hard to understand what could have frightened two grown men for half a century.

Er er ba is 2 2 8 in Chinese. It stands for a day 2-28 or February 28, 1947. By losing World War II Japan gave up control over Taiwan on September 2nd, 1945 under order No.1 from Japanese General Head Quarters. In October, twelve thousand military personnel and two hundred officials of the Nationalist Chinese Republican government landed on the island.[42] As with the transfer of power to the Manchus hundreds of years before, the coming of the Chiang government, one might have thought, would end further debate as to whether Taiwan was a part of China but the opposite happened yet again.

Initially, the Taiwanese welcomed the Chinese but their opinion rapidly soured soon after the undisciplined rag tag remnants of the army, locked in a life and death struggle with the mainland communists, arrived. The mainlanders viewed the long separated Taiwanese as traitors and the Taiwanese soon viewed the mainlander in the same light as earlier brutish Manchu officials. To make matters worse, the economy was turned up side down by the sudden influx of immigrants, which began to pour in as the communists gained momentum on the mainland.

The Taiwanese saw their lands go from boom under the Japanese to bust overnight culminating in rice shortages never before experienced by the Taiwanese. Raw material was requisitioned for the war effort with the communists and inflation soon skyrocketed. It was natural for the people to compare the new government to the disciplined and orderly Japanese predecessors. Chiang's representative on Taiwan Chen Yi made sure all vital positions in government as well as civilian life fell into the hands of the newly arrived mainlander and the ROC government began a campaign to de-Japanese the people.

Governor –General Chen Yi could speak both Japanese and Taiwanese but he refused to conduct affairs of state in any language other than Mandarin Chinese. He expected Taiwanese to learn Mandarin Chinese.[43] Corruption ran rampant within the lopsided government and the unrest mounted as it had during the Manchu years. One colonial despot had simply replaced another in the eyes of the Taiwanese, a government that was making a misery out of their lives.

By er er ba, rebellion was riding a hot wave of kerosene in the air and all that was needed to set off an explosion was a small spark. The spark came in the form of a Taiwanese woman working as a street vendor selling contraband cigarettes. Six plainclothes policemen confiscated her operations and when she attempted to retrieve her goods they bashed her with the butt of a gun. A crowd attempted to intercede prompting the police to draw their guns. By the time it was done a bystander was killed.

The following day on February 28th, 1947 protestors took to the streets, shops and factories closed, and students went on strike.[44] Governor-General Chen Yi's reaction was predictable given his bias. On March 8, 1947, reinforcements from the hardened Nationalist troops arrived from the mainland with heavy weapons that were unleashed on the unarmed civilian population. Order was restored by the end of March after thousands of Taiwanese had been killed and many more tortured and imprisoned.

According to some estimates, as many as 28,000 people had been killed but numbers vary from 10,000 to 28,000. Virtually all of the local Taiwanese political leadership and intellectual elite were targeted and exterminated. Through the years, numerous others disappeared in the middle of the night never to be seen again to the torture chambers of Green Island. These were the events that had made an everlasting impression on my father and uncle.

It made such an impression on Dad that nearly fifty years later he still cannot talk about it. Even in America he feared KMT assassins would come knocking at his door as if they could read his mind from thousands of miles away, and it is the reason he chose to keep his children in the dark. Such was the brutality of the "white terror" that killed a whole generation of prominent Taiwanese.

In the years that followed the KMT's KGB like machine, the Taiwan Garrison Command effectively crushed any voice of dissent on the island by assassination or imprisonment. Green Island, located off the southeast coast of Taiwan adjacent to Taitung, remains as one of the last few standing reminders of the thousands of "prisoners of conscience" that suffered at the hands of the KMT. Ironically, former survivors of the gallows now want to make the site a tourist attraction or, as a survivor Mr. Huang points out, a place where "people will more or less get educated by accident."[45]

As a result of his eight years as a political prisoner on Green Island, writer Bo Yang developed the opinion "which is that in the past 5,000 years the Chinese people lived without dignity. The justice in China is the darkest in the world. In our tradition there is no tradition of human rights." He was at the forefront of fighting to make the jail, inappropriately named Oasis Village, a memorial. Although the memorial is planned to have six hundred names of former prisoners etched onto a monument, estimates calculate that 20,000 more will need to be added.[46]

Legislator Shih Ming-teh started his 25 years of imprisonment at age 21. During his life sentence he spent 13 years in solitary confinement and was force-fed over 3,000 times during his hunger strikes. The former DPP chairman reflects, "Life is unpredictable." Advocates of the monument, such as Peter Huang director for the Taiwan Association of Human Rights, see the project as only a small step in the governments "recognition of the White Terror in the past and also Taiwan's future commitment to human rights." Huang adds, "Eventually, the government will have to take more than symbolic measures to protect human rights here."[47]

It should be noted that Green Island is just one of many detention sites employed by the KMT. The White Terror effectively pacified the 90 percent Taiwanese population. Today KMT mainlanders still comprise only about 15% of the population. The KMT saw their methods as the necessary means to continue the fight with the communists and maintain their assertion of a *one China policy* under the KMT. These were the times that prompted Mom and Dad to become Americans.

The one China policy that peppers the newspapers today was born out of the KMT war with the communists. The Taiwanese adopted the policy by coincidence for Taiwan became the last outpost for Chiang's retreat. To military historians, it is a wonder how Chiang managed to lose the war against the communists. Superior in numbers, supplies, money and backed by the technological might of the Americans, victory seemed assured. However, Chiang lost by overextending his army even as American advisor repeatedly implored him not to, stubbornly fixating on extermination campaigns while trying to hold onto vast tracks of territory. Furthermore, the brutality of his extermination campaigns and the alienation of the common people proved to be his undoing. His army proved at times to be undisciplined, corrupt and ambiguous as to their loyalties. These were the same qualities that endeared them to the Taiwanese in the early years of their occupation.

By the end of the affair, the Americans were all but ready to wash their hands of the Chiang debacle but the beginning of the Korean War changed everything. The Korean War re-polarized the world into the bi-polar struggle with communism and America reasserted its commitment to Chiang by dispatching the navy to patrol the Taiwan Straits. The American Navy bought Chiang crucial time and insured that the communist would not mount a successful invasion of the island. Taiwan was granted a seat in the United Nations as the true representative of all of China, a play acted out and believed by some even today. With the rise of the communists on the mainland the effective end of Republican China came to a close. The idea of Republican China had been a bumpy road starting at the end of the last imperial dynasty of China under the Ching on 10 October 1911. The day is observed on Taiwan as a holiday called 'Double Tenth' marking the beginning of Dr. Sun Yat-sen first provisional presidency of the People's Republic of China. It did not last long and what followed was a virtual period of warlordism where no power on the continent was able to unite the country until the communists established the People's Republic of China (PRC) in 1949. From then on, there have been two Chinas.

It is important to note the familiar, recurrent Chinese theme that shaped the communist mainlander psyche as a result of the epic struggle during the period of warlordism. Like the Manchus and, the Ming before, the Communists set about closing their borders and focusing inward in their attempt to preserve the land, culture and to consolidate power. China has been a closed, inward-looking society for many centuries now and has lost its place as a dynamic environment for innovation. On the other hand, Taiwan has a long history of adaptation to change making it well suited for the importation and exportation of new ideas. As a result, by 1984 the small island was the tenth largest exporting and the fifteenth largest trading nation in the world with two-way trade totaling $52.4 billion dollars.[48] China seeks to regain its prominence but the inertia of having been closed for so long is difficult to overcome.

China's cycle of paranoia concerning outside forces of invasion explain the nearly hysterical reactions of its government when it comes to matters of internal security, such as with the recent American spy plane incident at Hainan island. The same can be said about the issue of Taiwanese independence, which China feels is an internal affair.

Chinese can readily remember the arrival of the Portuguese in 1516, which led to a trading post at Macau. By the time the Ching dynasty was in power the West had embarked on a land-grabbing spree that carved China up into 'spheres of influence. Indo-China, Vietnam, Laos, Cambodia, Burma (Myanmar), Korea were all relieved from Chinese suzerainty. The Japanese forced China to cede Taiwan.

The greatest cultural assimilator in history to that point was quickly becoming assimilated. The humiliation was complete and both the Communists and the Chiang led Nationalists fought for years to restore Chinese control of the mainland against outside forces as well as among themselves. It is a testament to the diversity among the people of China that it took such a brutal effort to unite the country within a common ideology. In any event, the past has set the stage for the dialogue that continues till today over the issue of Taiwan.

The opulence of the Chiang Kai-shek memorial speaks to the far more familiar story of the Generalissimo. The giant blue octagonal roof that serves as the centerpiece of the quadrangle soars to a height of 76 meters and is a constant reminder of the wealth accumulated on the island since the end of World War II. Underneath the blue tiled roof, the memorial hall entrance is framed by a massive Ming styled arch towering 30 meters (100 feet) high and 76 meters (250) feet across. We walk through the immense sea of stone lining the quadrangle; the Antaean buildings surrounding us resemble artificial mountains ringing a stone valley. It would be remiss if we did not mention and give credit to the economic miracles that the Chiang regime preformed. The small island of Taiwan has evolved into an economic tiger on the world stage.

"Would we have prospered less under the Japanese?" Dad asks.

It is a question that cannot be answered and most historians agree that credit is deserved for the Chiang regime starting with his sweeping land reforms. But even this is a problem for my father. Chiang Kai-shek nationalized the family lands that were the legacy to my mother from Koxinga and redistributed them. Although they paid for the land in what they thought was fair at the time, the same land a decade later would be worth an astronomical multiplication of its acquired price. This does not sit well on my father's abacus.

As a result, the Chiang garden outside the memorial is ripe with Asian pines and evergreens. The pond is thick with carp over-fed by kind tourists all paid for from funds that may have rightfully been others. Whether Chiang is viewed as a hero or a murderer depends on who you ask and what their past affiliations were. Each has their version of history. It also depends which generation you ask.

I do not harbor the kind of feeling that lie at the core of my father and his contemporaries. I have thought more in my life about Abraham Lincoln than I have about Chiang Kai-shek. It illustrates the gulf in life experiences between the past generation and mine. There is a significant generation gap between young and old as well on Taiwan.

Chiang did manage to salvage the remnants of portions of the Imperial culture of China and managed to keep the island out of the hands of the communists determined to rewrite all of Chinese history. He was a man created by his time, a time of chaos and the vacuum of leadership. An ignoble time in China dominated by the humiliating occupation of foreign powers on the mainland.

The dark side of Chiang's legacy is far less known owning to the fact that the authorities in power until recent history sought to erase this chapter-but the Taiwanese people have forgotten nothing. The argument will rage on, and I will have to wait for a visit to the Koxinga Shrine for my Amy Tan moment.

For many Taiwanese, Chiang's fight with the communists was never their fight. For many Taiwanese, their struggle has always been for self-determination, having say in the direction of where their island was headed, and finally they do. They have it just in time for the communists to declare a new holy war on Taiwan. They have it just in time for the rest of the world to once again ignore them so as not to alienate the big red star. How redundant is that?

The unimaginable happened in Taiwan in 2000. For the first time in its history there was a peaceful transfer of power through a *true two party election*. Threatened with the prospect of a declaration of independence from a newly elected party, the communist Chinese proceeded to mass troops along the Taiwan Straits and rattle sabers with talk of Taiwanese annihilation should this happen. The elections went off peacefully and the KMT was summarily voted out of office with a new party president elected. Chen Shui-bian of the Democratic progressive Party, who has openly endorsed independence in the past, was placed into power. Since the Chinese exercises in the straits, Chen Shui-bian has toned down his independence rhetoric.

As amazing as the events of the past year were, none of these events would have happened without the stewardship of former President Lee Teng-hui. Lee Teng-hui was hand picked by Chiang Kai-shek son Chiang Ching-kuo to lead the KMT after his death. The main difference with Lee is that he was the first Taiwanese born President of the island and advocated native Taiwanese rights. The seat of power was to take a major historical revision of the perspective of the past.

Not surprisingly, he also advocated an abandonment of the KMT philosophy of one-China for the independence that has eluded Taiwan for millennia. His family history is the same as my families and he sought higher education at Cornell University in the United States just like my parents did at NYU. You could say that Lee Teng-hui is the father of modern Taiwan even as his critics deride him as Mr. IBM, "international big mouth" for his beliefs. An article in the March 25, 2000 *Washington Post* describes Lee's contributions as such:

"Twelve years ago, this island languished in an identity crisis. People wondered if they were Chinese, Taiwanese, Hakka or Min-nan. Today, the overwhelming majority of Taiwanese share a sense of belonging to an independent nation with an identity distinct from that of China. Over the 12 years he has ruled this island, with his trademark steel-wool hair and immutable smile, Lee has helped create a country.

Lee has used his success in developing a national identity to establish a powerful consensus on Taiwan's approach toward Beijing, making the island less ready to simply melt into China. Last year, in stating that China and Taiwan should establish "special state-to-state" relations, Lee defined terms of negotiations that will outlast his rule.

"His whole idea really surrounds on core vision—to build Taiwan as an independent sovereign state and to prevent the possibility that Taiwan would succumb to Beijing's unification schemes," said Chu Yun-han, a political scientist at National Taiwan University. "He put that vision before anything else."

Lee also is being followed into office by a man who more than any other candidate adheres closely to his views on China and Taiwan. Chen Shui-bian used to be an independence activist. Under pressure from Beijing, which is threatening war if Taiwan declares independence, and the United States, which is considered unlikely to defend Taiwan if it takes that step, Chen has modified his views.

Today, Taiwan is careful about rhetoric, for or against independence, as it sits next to a sleeping giant with nuclear rockets in his pocket. What evolved in Taiwan is ironically a quantum leap back towards what the Confucian scholars professed. It only took 5,000 years to evolve. The Confucian value that, "Government is merely setting things right" is finally practiced on the island. Perhaps, this is what Chiang Kai-shek really had in mind. The island appears today to mirror the Confucian value of "the rule of government by the people for the people."

I do not share my father's disdain for Chiang Kai-shek because after all, I am an American and my parents protected me from learning their troubles. I do not feel what they feel. But, I would not find my grand homecoming today at the memorial. My compass points me south. Ready to embrace my heritage. I am ready to feel the warm tropical embrace from the land where we had lived as kings. I was ready to be healed by the legacy of Kuo Hsing-yeh.

James Yu, As I Thought- June 1977

I can't believe 5th grade is over. It sure took its time getting here, then bam! I really don't know what's the big deal about school anyways. This is the first grade I've ever finished from September to June and I didn't learn nearly as much as watching T.V. Old people are always saying how bad T.V. is, but its not.

My sister Rowena can't get through a sentence without saying "fuck this fuck that, did you see that fucking guy?" As far as I can tell she learned to speak like that in school. At least I can get through a sentence without saying fuck!

Besides, I've been way to busy to go to school ever since kindergarten. I've seen the real world out there and you don't learn none of it in school. I can tell you all there is to know about airports, bus stations, train stations and motels. They don't teach you in school how to catch a plane to Tokyo or Taipei. I suppose that's pretty important stuff if ya want to go somewheres.

Theres a lot of bullcrap in school too. But I don't hate it. Pretzel time, thumbs up seven up and recess is pretty cool. T.V. is boring during school hours anyway so I'm not missing nothing. You might wonder how I've become such a reconessieur about T.V., I used to watch about 14 hours a day when we were on the run. It was kinda my job back then.

It all started about five years ago when I was a kid. Mom and Dad were always changing their minds back then, and it wasn't about a few weeks had passed that they told me to "pack up you bags" again. I was going back to Taiwan this time for goods. Dad said, "we can no longer afford America."

I don't know exactly what he's talking about cause we've been flying all over the planet since then and that can't be cheaper than staying in one spot. I've got spoons from Air Siam, Northwest Orient, China Air, Pan Am, Air Nippon, Singapore Air, American, United, TWA, Allegheny, Air Canada and more. I'm kinda attached to them and I don't let anybody eat with them. They just sit in a rusty tin box and start to smell bad. My set weighs about ten pounds. They've been with me all my life.

Well when Mom said "pack your bags," we're headed for Taiwan, I said "I don't wanna," but it didn't do much good. I just ended up stuffing as much of my life into a blue suitcase that was twice as big as me. I can carry the suitcase all by myself. I've had to lug it all over Asia. I couldn't get enuff of my stuff in that baby blue suitcase, though, and Mom threw out the rest. I told her I hated her guts but that didn't help either. My stuff still went down the incinerator.

I suppose every thing I have in the world fits into that case. That blue suitcase is kinda my own portable closet. I've lived out of it for five years now. Whenever we move somewhere, I don't bother unpacking.

It was a good thing my scabs on my butt had plopped off by the time we flew out of JFK back home in New York cause the flight to Taipei took forever. It turned dark and then light again and we still weren't there. Someone told me I lost a day but that doesn't make any sense to me. How can you lose a day? Airplanes are funny, one sec your sweating like a pig and they next your freezing to death. But the food is great and the stewardesses give you as much as you want. It was still kinda hard to sit on my butt without scratching all the time. I wasn't happy about havin to go back to crapping in a hole again.

By the time we landed in Taipei, no one around us was in a good mood except Dad. I think he was happy to leave his boarded up shop on Kapok Street behind him. The last time I saw it someone had spray painted *GO HOME DIRTY CHINK SHOP* over the wood sheets over the windows. I don't know why they did that cause everybody I ever met loved the shop full of candles, incense, beaded curtains, and greeting cards. I loved playing in that shop full of back scratchers, inflatable ducks, and mooing boxes. I guess most of the stuff Dad sold was junk, maybe that's why someone was pissed at him.

By the time we met Rupert and Rowena at the gate even Dad was in a shitty mood. Rupert and Rowena were as green as frogs and Rupert kept yelling, "when are we going home?" Rup kept buzzing around Dad like a fly. Dad wasn't smiling any more.

Rup yelled, "I'm not going to be a part of the Yu family relocation program!"

Well Rup shouldn't of said that cause the next thing we heard was a big whaap, whaap, whapp! Dad just started whaling on Rup right there in the middle of the airport. I couldn't believe my eyes. I'd never seen Dad hit anyone before and Mom and everyone just stood and you could here a pin drop. Rup was crawled up in a ball on the floor and Rowena just stared up at Dad with a blank look that she always has on her face these days.

Rup didn't say a word after that and he hasn't ever said a kind word to Dad since. It was hotter than hell in Taipei. Nothing had changed. We moved right in with Auntie again and you could just tell they were happy as clams about that. Dad and Auntie were always arguing about something. Mom says, "it's adult business," but Rup says it's all about money. Rup says a lot of nasty things about old people and especially about Dad. He back talks to Dad whenever he gets the chance and runs for Mom's protection before Dad can flatten him.

Eventually, Mom and Dad found a place for us to live and we paid off Auntie I guess. By the time we said our good-byes, they were about ready to kick us out the door.

The last thing Auntie said to Dad was "they like to fight and not fit in." Dad slapped Rup on the back of the head for that which started Mom on a screaming fit. Rup was cowering behind Mom as Dad and Mom began screaming their heads off in three different languages. I caught fuck this and fuck that in all three languages, maybe that's where Rowena gets some of it. I don't know why I have such a clean mouth.

I never saw Auntie's family again and I guess they never invited us over.

Well it didn't get any better having our own place in the Kowloong Apartment tower. Mom, Dad, Rup and Rowena were always screaming about something. Even baby Carolyn started screaming too. We still weren't going to school and we didn't even have a T.V. Can you imagine not having a T.V. Life was just pure hell.

We were pretty lucky to get a place in the new fangled Kowloong tower though. Our cement house was one of the fancy new ones they were building all over the place. It was pretty fun to climb up to the roof, which was way up there in the sky. You could see the mountains and all the ants doing their laundry on the rooftops below. We even had electricity and indoor plumbing, but still no toilet. We still crapped in a hole that was made out of porcelain.

It was just our luck that the place would burn down to the ground. It burned down only six months after we moved in. Dad said it blew up like "a Roman candle." Rowena was the first one to notice the smell. Pretty soon you could hardly miss it. The whole apartment smelled like it does when they tar the streets outside. I looked out the window and saw people jumping out from the floors below. Mom and Dad are screaming at each other like crazed dogs.

Mom shouts, "how could you have let this happen?"

Dad curses her back telling her to "go to hell."

Rup and Rowena are shouting, "what the fuck are we going to do?" But Mom and Dad are too busy cussing each other out.

Mom says, "you're a rotten bastard, you're a failure, and the biggest baby in the family."

Dad raises his hand to strike her but he stops. I've never seen him hit her, but he seems to take it out on Rup instead.

Screw this I think. It's every Yu for himself. While everyone else is still screaming at each other, I open the apartment door and cotton candy thick, black smoke rushes into the apartment. I hold my breath. The walls of the hallway are hot but I feel my way over to the stairs and run down the pitch-black shaft as fast as my little legs will carry me. It's kind of surprising how easy it is to hold your breath while running down fifteen flights of stairs in the pitch dark when you have too. Opening the door to the outside hurt my eyes more than jumpin into the darkness. It was bright and sunny outside.

When I turned around, I was surprised to see Rowena and baby Carolyn in Dad's arms right behind me.

"Where's Mom," I asked?

Dad looked up at our window.

"Rups still with her," Rowena said.

It didn't take long before Rup and Mom had to crawl out onto the ledge to get away from the smoke and flames that were shooting out the windows all around them. They clung to each other like Koala bears. Rup and Mom always take the same side ever since they crawled out on that ledge together.

Firemen and people were barking at them to hold on, hold on, but I was sure they were dead! I could see Mom getting weaker by the second and she just couldn't hold on to Rup and the building much longer. Mom's a tiny lady, five foot-two or three. The second she let her grip relax Rup started to slip like Wiley coyote spinning his wheels before a fall. He went end over end and I yelled at my brother but I don't even remember what I said. He smashed into the crane below legs first and that saved his life. The firemen had lifted it up as high as it would go and it caught him. Mom came soaring down after him like a barefoot bat out of hell with a huge crunching sound.

I don't remember anything about that day from then on except that I peed in my pants, which dried as hard as cardboard. I don't know when your supposed to stop wearing diapers but I still kind of wear them and I'm about to start Junior High School. I don't actually wear diapers of course but sometimes, I stuff toilet paper in them if I feel like I need some extra soaking up down there. Sometimes I wet my pants and there isn't nothing I can do about it. I usually know when it's coming though and I do my own laundry so nobody needs to know about it.

Mom and Rup spent a couple of days in the hospital but it wasn't long before they joined us at the hotel and started yelling and screaming with Dad again. Dad didn't yell back as much cause he probably felt bad for leaving them behind like he did. Well Mom and Dad are always changing their minds anyway. They don't much agree on nothing.

I think Mom blamed him for the whole fire and everything. Dad said the papers said, "faulty wiring burned down the Kowloong building." That's no news flash to me! Even the brand spanking new buildings got wire threaded all over the place like a million hairballs. Every time we plugged in a rice cooker the lights would go brown. Our neighbors have about a jillion electronic things plugged into a socket on their balcony where it rains.

"This would have never happened in an American building," Dad said. I don't know why that is but I believe him.

So, Mom and Dad decided to forget new fangled high-rise living and we moved into a two-story cement box on the side of some hill in Tienmu.

I guess I couldn't read or write so good back then cause in 1974 they decided I needed to go back to school. Up till then, I'd finished about half of kindergarten, a couple of weeks of first grade when I'd returned to New York and just about none of the second grade. I don't think you learn anything in those grades cause I mostly missed them and it aint hurt me none. There was no way I could learn Chinese fast enuff to go to public school so their only choice was to put me into Taipei American School. They let me just waltz right into the third grade there and I was having fun for awhile.

Taipei American school cost an arm and a leg if you weren't a military brat or an embassy brat. It was worth every penny to me to be around people who could talk English. They shipped us in on bullet shaped yellow busses like privileged guest through the hot, sticky loud mess that was Taipei to this fenced compound that had all the air-conditioning and hamburgers you could ask for. Taipei

American school was like a piece of America surrounded by a brown, black-haired ghetto. At school, chairs and tables were miraculously stacked and cleaned each day, the carpet was clean enuff to eat off, and pencil sharpeners were at just the right height for me. The bathrooms always had toilet paper in them, we got two squares a day, and I even had a box with my name on it where stuff would appear like magic. It was the first time that I ever loved school.

I'd go just for the food and air-conditioning alone. Things were starting to look up and I scrubbed my day clothes just as happy as can be in a 30" diameter galvanized bowl cause I wanted to look nice for school. The bricks of soap I used could burn a hole through your hands if you let them sit but they did the trick and my T-shirts dried up stiff as taco shells.

Sometimes, the water left a little red tint to your underwear cause the tank holding the rainwater on the roof was rusting away. But all in all life was looking up and I even got to go swimming with Dad at the Grand Hotel one day and went to a movie every now and then at west gate. I even had a few friends who were kids of old patriots from home. Mom called them ex-patriots. One of the good things that was kind of bad too was that I almost never saw Dad anymore. I don't know what or where he was most of the time. I missed him but when he was gone there was at least peace and quiet at home. I was kind of getting used to the heat too and I even kind of liked the nearby mountains and palm trees blowing in the wind.

Just about when I was as pleased as I could be, partway through my first semester, Mom rustled me out of my sleep in the middle of the night and whispered to me "start packing James were going on a trip."

"I gotta go to school tomorrow," I says and konked out.

The second time she woke me Rup, Rowena and Carolyn were all dressed and ready to head out somewheres. I saw my baby blue suitcase in a pile at the door. Mom picked me up and the next thing I know I was in a taxi headed for downtown.

"What about school," I asked?

Mom just gave me a stare and thirty minutes later we rustled into a cold, furniture-less, one bedroom concrete box under a neon

Foremost milk sign. Dad came home to an empty apartment. Mom had kidnapped us for the first time. The first night we all slept on the floor. Rup commandeered the only room and I couldn't even go in it without him throwing me on my head. I think he thought he was the new big shot around here. He is four years older than me and I would never win any fights with him. We lived off the bare cement floor for the next couple of weeks. There was no place to go and nothing to do all day long and we spent hours just laying around moaning and bashing each other. Sometimes we roamed the alleys around the apartment but there were no kids around this industrial place and the only thing to do was to go to the street vendors to buy dehydrated plums when we had money.

After two months of this Mom said, "pack our bags," again and she didn't have to tell me twice. We waited all day for something to happen and we waited half the night for her to come home. We were starved to death and when she came home we clawed over each other to get to some food. I ended up with a quarter bun and passed out from the fight.

When I woke up the next day Mom said "unpack your bags."

"What the fuck is going on," Rowena yelled at Mom!

"You just better shut up!" Mom yelled back.

"I'm going to go get some more food so just wait and keep your mouse shut," she said.

"Mouth, Mom, its mouth not mouse," I said.

"Aiiiya!" she said.

We spent week after week with the same routine. Get up in the morning and wait for Mom to come back with food at night. I could hear my stomach growling all day and I would tear at my hair in frustration. That's when I got the idea in my head that I was going to run away. When I get an idea stuck up there it aint over till it's unstuck.

"What if Mom doesn't come back?" Rowena asked.

"Who cares," I would say, "we're gonna starve to death anyway." And so I just waited for the right day.

One day Mom said "we need to go to the immigration office," or we would be kicked outta Taiwan and have no place at all to live. So we all jumped into a Taxi and it was really nice to get away from that cement cell.

Mom said our "tourist visas were about to expire." Tourist visas, I thought we was Taiwanese? I guess we couldn't afford Taiwan neither cause they was trying to kick us out. The taxi dropped us out onto a boulevard as wide as a 747 landing strip downtown and we nearly got squashed trying to get across. I've learned the best way is to make a run as fast as you can for the cement island in the middle and then choose your best bet to dash across the other side but Mom hasn't figured it out yet. You would have thought she'd have figured it a long time ago since she comes from here but she hasn't. She tip toes her way across there as cars whizz by her honking their horns and swerving all over the place with baby Carolyn in her arms and Ruppert holding her hand.

Rowena's figured it out though and she and I were waitin on the other side and we could barely stand to watch. She just leaves it all to the cars as to whether they squash her or not and these folks drive like they don't give a damn bout nothing. I started thinking Mom's not carrying a full deck.

There must a been a heck of a sale on immigration on the day we got to the office cause it looked like Woolworth's on Christmas eve. People were lined up in rows stretching all the way out into the street. A lot of folks were in a big hurry to go somewheres. We waited for three hours before we finally got to the front of the line but when we got there Mom said we was in the wrong line and we had to get in another one. So we went out in the hot sun again and laid out on the cement and kicked each other around on the ground. When we got to the part of the line inside again it wasn't much cooler even with the fans up high cranking away, but the floor was a lot cooler. Ladies had their own hand held fans which I thought was smart but Rup said their making themselves hotter by fanning themselves.

I was wondering why adults were so stupid cause there were hundreds of them fanning themselves away. Another couple of hours later we made it to the front of the line again and the only thing I could think of was water. It had taken us about six hours to move forty yards. Well it wasn't long before Mom and the black haired teller with a part in the middle were yelling at each other in Taiwanese. Mom was working up a lather around her mouth and I had a hunch we were in for some more bad news.

"James," Mom kept saying, "his name is James Yu" in Chinese.

"Bushi!" the teller says. "Tai, Tai, dui buqi," he says pointing to the huge line behind us.

"Aiiya!" Mom says. She keeps shoving our passports in his face but he just keeps wagging his greasy head and pointing to the people behind us. After about ten minutes of this the people behind us are starting the grumble and start shoving us around. It's starting to get a little scary to me.

Mom says "I've got to give you all Chinese names right now."

"What are you talking about, what's wrong with the names we got?" Rowena asks.

"That man says we can't have Be-co-lan names cause were Chinese people. He says our surname is Yu so we have to have Chinese names."

"Meiguo ren," Mom barks at the teller, "we're Americans!"

"Bushi, Tai, Tai!" he yells back and pounds his hand into the desk.

Well you don't need to speak Chinese to figure out what he was saying. Hanging out with Mom, I think I learned all the bad Chinese words first like *kong tai* which as far as I can tell means knucklehead in Chinese.

Mom finally gives in and puts her hand on Ruppert's head and says "Pang Ying." She put her hand on Rowena's head and says "Chyong Ing," then me "Ting Kuei" and then Carolyn "Hsiu Ying." Mom gave Ruppert her brother's name, me grandpa's name, Rowena grandma's name and baby Carolyn her younger sister's name.

"This is bullshit," Rup says and he starts to storm out of the office.

Well this seemed to me the perfect opportunity to run away if there ever was one. I slipped away after Rup and by the time I saw Mom and the rest of the family walk out the door I was across the 747 landing strip and three huge city blocks away.

The truth is I could have run away on any day that Mom left us at the house but I had no idea where that part of town was and how to find what I was looking for. From downtown I was pretty sure I could find my way back to Dad and our old apartment in the hills. I'd gone downtown to watch movies a dozen times and I even knew the bus number that would take me back.

It was pretty fun running around the streets for the first couple of hours trying to figure out where I was. It was harder than I thought, though, and every time I thought I recognized a landmark it turned out to be wrong. I was in a part of town that was like an elevated city with cement skybridges connecting other parts of the city for miles. The place is something out of a sci-fi movie with shops and sidewalks in the sky. I passed by about a jillion coin shops and ceramic shops that all seem to sell the same stuff. By the time I found a stairwell to take me down to the street level it was dark outside and I was completely lost. It didn't help to have all those noodle shops and restaurants stinking up the street and churning up the acids in my tummy.

It was getting cold too. It always surprised me how cold it got at night in Taipei when the days were like being in an oven. I only had on a pair of cotton shorts and T-shirt with a cartoon basketball man on it. I walked and walked till somethin told me I wasn't going to walk no more and then I crawled up into a ball underneath one of those skybridge stairs and fell asleep. Eventually, the shivering woke me up and I had no idea how long I had been out. I didn't like people starring at me so I started to walk again just one foot in front of the next. I hadn't eatin since our breakfast ammoyya and my pockets were full a nothin but cotton bunnies.

When I walked up to a crowd around a noodle vendor he shouted "qu!" at me and I got the hint. It was better to walk fast cause it was warmer that way and it didn't really matter what direction I was headed cause I'd given up. I don't know how late it was but the crowds kept getting bigger and bigger on the streets and pretty soon there were people elbow to elbow. It was kinda nice and warm around all those people.

After I'd walked about an hour I finally figured out why there were so many folks around me. All the neon and huge murals stared down on me and it soon hit me that I was in movie row! For the first time that night I felt a gush of hope. I started to try to retrace my steps back to my Dad and home. The first mile was a synch and I even saw one of the number 11 busses pass by, but as I got to the outskirts of town I got turned around again and ended walking out into some rice paddies. I don't know how far I went but when I woke up the next morning I was covered in water buffalo fertilizer. There was nothing around me but wide open fields for as far as I could see and I knew then and there that I was never gonna find Dad.

"Where are you Dad?" I whispered. I hate to admit it but I started to cry like a wussy. Okay, but not too much. So I decided I was going to back track my way into town and start over. I passed a bunch of farmers riding on water buffalo powered carts full of straw and I never saw such rude stares before. Those country idiots got no manners at all. It was just the opposite in the city. People didn't even want to notice me even though I stunk something awful. I guess city people got better manners. I saw a little leftovers in a bowl of noodles in a shop on the road and I snuck over and grabbed a handful and kept walking.

By the time I backtracked to Movie row it was hot as hell again and around noontime. I had to lay down again cause my whole body got clammy and cold even though I could feel my insides burning me up. When I woke up I decided it was time to try a new strategy cause I was starving to death. I started back tracking my way to the immigration office and I was surprised at how easy it was to find it. I figured that I had just as good a chance of finding Mom as finding Dad and Mom's place was a hell of a lot closer. I could remember the taxi ride in pretty good and there were only about a dozen streets that I could go down from the bus terminal that I knew how to get to. I was just gonna go down every one of them as far as I could until I found the place.

I went down all the wrong ones until I started to recognize stuff again, and it took me the whole day and night. When I was sure I was on the right road I fell asleep again in a stairway up to a shop. I woke up to a bunch of chickens clucking all over the place around me and when I saw the Foremost Milk sign I knew I had found my way back. It was about four in the afternoon three days after I had left this place.

I didn't even need to knock on the door cause Mom opened it before I even got there and gave me a big hug. Five minutes later I was asleep and I didn't wake up until noon the next day. I ate just about everything we had in the house and that wasn't much but it turned out to be too much.

I learned its not good to not eat for a couple of days and then eat until your full. Cause when I did eat, I got the worst burning Hershey squirts that I ever had. I can't quite describe it but the closest I can come is like if someone shoved a sword out your ass from inside your stomach. But that doesn't quite do it. It hurt so much I would pass out. But even that wasn't gonna stop me from eaten. I just couldn't help myself. It took me about a month to get my insides all worked out again.

In the meantime, Mom decided to let me in on her little secret. She could've saved her little secret cause I wasn't about to try running away again.

Mom said, "it's time we went home to America." I guess she was expecting a big thank you very much from me but I think what I was thinking was *finally.*

Mom added, "but first we need to get the money to do it."

"We don't have a cent," I said.

"No, we can do it," she said. "I've been talking to grandpa but he hasn't given me the money yet. Soo, I think we need to go down and ask him for it in person," she said. "We're never coming back to this place, James," she said.

Well that was all I needed to hear and I did give her a big thank you very much and didn't want to ever let go of her. A couple of days later, we were on a train to Tainan and she was right, we never went back to that place.

I guess, we were kind of a site to grandpa in old Tainan. We were kinda wasted away looking and I guess Mom was pretty smart to parade us around in front of him like that. He growled at his servants to feed us and keep it comin. With three or four squares it took us just days to get our spirits up and pretty soon we were running up and down the halls of grandpa's huge Japanese styled mansion like a pack of wild jungle boars. Mom said, "watch out for those 1,000 year old heirlooms," but she was always one step to slow. Even old gramps was fair game as we ran over his old boats. One day Rowena kicked me through a rice paper partition that separated the living room from the sitting room. The servants hated our guts and they held their breath every time we even grazed old gramps with a kung fu kick. I think they thought we were crazy and about to get our arms and legs chopped off for even touching such a powerful distinguished man. I guess gramps used to be the mayor of Tainan and Mom has always bragged about how her Mom is descended from some famous pirate named Koxinga. What the hell do we care? He's just an old man who gets in our way.

Anyway, gramps loves us. Every time he sees us kicking the shit out of each other you can tell he's laughin his ass off. When I start mimicking drunken master, crane fighter, tiger fist gramps can't keep back the smiles. His servants who follow him around and attend to his every move can't believe their eyes.

The one time I heard him burst out into laughter was when we played *Revenge of the Flying Guillotine*. The movie was about some cut throat assassins who went around chopping off the heads of people they didn't like with a secret weapon. Their weapon was a Frisbee like basket attached to a rope, which would slam shut like a camera lens when they pulled on it. Usually they'd just give the basket head and all to the family of their enemies.

We made a bunch of these guillotines out of hats and when we started launching them at each other gramps just about lost his lunch. Gramps kinda sounds like a donkey when he laughs. Well, to make a long story short we had our money in short of a month. This musta pissed off his servants and his mistress who Mom says are "still sticking around looking for their big pay day."

"They still think he's some sort of king," Rup said.

He looks like some old guy about to die to me, and I guess I shouldn't of said that cause he did die two years later and I never saw him again. Gramps wasn't such a fierce guy I thought. He even kissed me once when I sat in his lap.

"He's the last of his kind," Mom said when he passed away, "the last of the Ming warlords."

I wish old gramps could've got away from his sour group of servants and visited us in the states. I think we could've had a ball. That's all I remember about old gramps Yeh Ting Kuei. I never met Mom's mom Liu Chyong Ing cause she died young, except now in Taiwan I had gramps name and Rowena had grandma's name.

Life As A Modern Bedouin, As I Thought In 1975-1977

You know it doesn't matter where you are you can learn how to be an American if you just watch enough T.V. You know I learned the Pledge of Allegiance, and all about George Washington, and The Declaration of Independence and all that but you can even get that on the boring PBS channel. What makes me extra-specially American is that I watch more than 10 hours a day. In America that's a job!

When we landed at the Honolulu airport, Ruppert kissed the ground like he'd been back from the moon or something. The first thing I noticed was how clean everything is in America. I think everything is better in America. I think that's part of being American too is you gotta be better than everybody else. I'm sure glad to be home but I'm not sure how I'm gonna be better than anybody?

You know T.V.'s pretty good in Japan too. We stopped by at my Uncle Richard's house in Tokyo and I just couldn't get enough of their giant robot cartoons. I kinda thought Japan was pretty clean too but everything is so crowded there, kinda minaturerized. That's another thing about America is you gotta be bigger than everybody else. Bigger is definitely better. You don't just eat chicken scraps chopped up and shared by the whole fricken family, you gotta eat a whole bucket of chickens from Churches Fried Chicken. And on-top-a that you gotta eat a whole carton of mushed potatoes with brown greasy stuff on-top-a that.

I love America!

You know when we got back I can't tell you how many months we stayed over in cheap motels with nothing to do but watch T.V. and that's okay with me cause they got all kinds of crazy shows on nowadays. In the morning they got cartoons like Bugs Bunny, Speed Racer, Felix the Cat, Magila Gorilla and after that they got old movies or game shows. I can't believe what they give away for free on *The Price is Right*. Man if we could just get on that show once we'd be set for life. There's so much stuff we don't have, I can't believe how much stuff we haveta buy.

Another thing about America that I learned from T.V. is that you gotta be a good guy. Bad guys are like scalping Indians, Japs, redcoats, Nazis, Mafiaososes. Good guys are like John Wayne, Robert Conrad, Captain America and Superman. Their always right and teaching those greasy bad guys a lesson.

By the time a got done watching old movies or gameshows, the soaps would come on. They stink!

I don't got nothin to say about them cause I don't think anybody watches them. We just leave them on for the noise and start bouncing on the beds and see who can hit the ceiling the fastest. Another great thing about motels is that you can do anything to em. You can just about turn em upways down and they send someone there the next day to clean up your mess. I'm never leaving America again, I don't care who tries to take me.

Sometimes we get so bored with the soaps we just fall asleep again and by the time we get up there's good stuff to watch again. Right around 3 o'clock is when all the really good stuff comes on. *The Brady Bunch, The Partridge Family, F-Troop, Hogan's Hero's, McHale's Navy, I Dream of Genie, Father Knows Best, Superman, Batman* and more. I figure you can learn just about all there is to know about being American right there.

Afternoon cartoons are better too. They got *The Jetsons, The Flinstones, Josie and the Pussycats, Scobby Doo, The Justice League, Spiderman* and more.

One day Mom says it's time we moved outta this motel so I said fine are we gonna have T.V. where we're going and she said "yeh, well buy a black and white," so that was okay by me.

So we moved into this luxury apartment on the seventeenth floor called the Kahala towers and it was the nicest place in the world. We had one bedroom for all four of us and my Mom, and that was plenty of room. We even had a terrace, which the natives around here call a lanai. Mom kept her word and bought us a 9" black and white and I was sure that we was Americans now. I don't think you can be American if you don't own a T.V.

Now I could stay up until midnight and watch all the late night shows like Love American Style, Sonny and Cher, Donny and Marie, and Johnny Carson. There is always something to watch on T.V. On Monday's they got football and on Saturdays and Sundays too. That's another thing. I think you gotta love football or at least baseball to be an American. You just gotta love beatin up on weaker, stupider people. They don't deserve to have nothing. But of course you gotta play fair like John Wayne.

Life was as good as can be except for one little thing.

Mom said, "don't ever let anybody know that you live here."

I said, "okay Mom but why?"

She said, "cause I said so, that's why!" and that was good enough for me.

Rup said, "you stupid little potato head your not even supposed to live here."

I said, "bullshit, you're the one that not supposed to live here."

"Fuck off, potato head," he said.

I don't know why but Rup just about hated my guts all of the time and I was always waitin for him to just throw me off the lanai.

I was trying not to but I was sorta crying a little and making it hard to watch T.V. but Rowena told me "I'm not supposed to be here either so don't worry."

I figured out a couple weeks later that only one child was allowed in a one-bedroom apartment but we had three to many. Rupert was the only one really allowed to be there and the rest of us was suppose to always sneak in. Well when I found that out I just quit talking to anyone in the building cause adults was always asking stupid questions. I tried to make myself invisible like the lady in the Fantastic Four.

The four of us would never enter the building at the same time and I got to wheres I could just about avoid anyone seeing me come in or out. Getting Carolyn into the building was special cause there wasn't supposed to be anybody her age in the building at all. Whenever she was havin a fit in the apartment we was just waitin for the police to bust down our door.

After a couple of weeks Mom decided the coast was clear enuff to try puttin me back in school. Luckily, school was just up the hill cause it woulda been hard to explain to some bus driver to drop me off a couple a blocks away everyday. It was actually kinda nice to cut back on my T.V. watching and that whole time the soaps was on was a waste anyway. I was really startin to enjoy what little I knew about school cause it was such a neat and tidy place usually.

Like I says before, I don't think you learn much in the 3rd grade either cause here I was now in the fourth and I'd missed most of the others. Fourth grade wasn't bad either. I learned about how to play the ukulele, how to say hello in Hawaiian that's aloha, and how to tell where I am on the island in Hawaiian. Makai is beach or south, Mauka is mountain or north, eva is toward Eva Beach or west and everyone knows Diamond Head is to the east. Bout the hardest thing is times tables which I aint paid no attention to yet cause it don't make no sense. I think that's about the only bad thing about school, times tables.

Well things was goin along just fine a pint of milk with cookies in the morning and a pint at lunch while playing marbles until the day I met Sean McDonald then things was never the same. Sean had long sandy brown and blond hair kinda straight as spaghetti like mine and we was best braas from the first day we met. We liked about just all the same things like marbles, football, comics, and Rockem, sockem robots. When he told me he had Rockem, Sockem robots that was that, I knew I had to go over to his house to play with em.

The problem with that is that Sean lived in the same building as me, only two floors down. I'd seen him and his Mom, who looks like

Cheryl Tieg with bigger tits about a jillion times, but I don't think they'd ever seen me. They weren't supposed to according to Mom. No one was supposed to know.

Well I don't care what Mom says when it comes to Rockem, Sockem robots, I'd seen the commercial enough to know that it was worth the risk. So one Saturday I said, "sure I'll come over."

Sean said, "my Mom will pick you up," and I says, "no thanks, I'll walk."

So there I was on a Saturday and Cheryl Tieg opens the door with a big old smile and says, "how'd you get in the building without buzzing up?"

"Eh..." That kinda stumped me but I woke up and say, "eh.., some old lady was comin out.".

"Oh," she says, "that's easy. Sean's watching T.V. in the living room," so I walk back into the apartment and the damn thing looks exactly the same as ours. I sit down right next to him and watch for about 5 minutes before he even notices me there.

"Jaaames," he says, "let me get my sockem robots," and we run into the room. Well time sure went fast and I don't know what time it was but Sean's Mom asked if we was "hungry for breakfast?" and we both said "yeh!" and came a running. I couldn't believe what they had for eatin down here.

The whole freakin table was full of pancakes, sausages, bacon, two kinds of eggs, toast, hand squeezed orange juice and more. Sean and his Mom couldn't believe how much I could eat but I told them they hadn't seen nothin yet.

Sean's Mom said, "are they feeding you at home?" and that kinda slowed me down a little.

Sean's Mom could've said anything to me and it wouldn't of bothered me though, cause I loved that Suzy Chapstick smile of hers and she could sure cook eggs.

I started visiting Sean all the time and I would even go downstairs so that they had to buzz me into the building. Mom didn't have a clue where I was and I couldn't tell you what she did with her time neither. Sean's mother was the nicest white person I had ever met and the only one that had ever paid me any attention before. She hugged me and let me sit on her lap and put her fingers through my hair and gave me kisses goodbye and Sean was like the brother I never had.

At night I dreamed about breakfast at Sean's house and wished they'd adopt me. Maybe it was all my fault cause all their good will kinda wished the truth right outta me. I was tired of lying to them all the time like some scamster. They was the nicest people I'd ever met and that includes family.

It was stupid of me to ride the elevator and I knew better than that. I guess it was my fault that Sean's Mom would eventually corner me one day.

"Hi Sweetie!" she said, "where ya been all my life?"

"Yay..a uhh," is all I could get outta my mouth and I could feel my stomach about to puke.

"Sean's at his father's right now?" she said. Did another old lady let you in?"

I couldn't say a thing.

"Are you feeling okay?" she said brushing my hair to the side. "Who do you know on seventeen?" she asked.

"I can't tell you," I said as my eyes fogged up. I swear sometimes I'm a wussy.

"It's okay hun," she said and gave me a kiss before she got out on her floor. It was kinda worse to be alone for the last two floors. When I got home I thought about jumpin off the lanai but that isn't quite me ya know. So I don't know why but I ended up downstairs knocking on Sean's door. Sean's Mom opened the door and just pulled me in and gave me the biggest hug and I started crying again in her arms like a big fat baby and I couldn't stand myself but her hug was the best thing I ever felt.

A few weeks later Mom said, "someone in the building has told the super about us and he wants us out."

It was time to pack our bags again. Super gave us a week to pack our bags or he would call the child social people but we lit out way before then. I'd known Sean and his Mom for four months but I would never see them again. They were the first white people I'd ever really got to know and love. We were on the run again and it was all my fault.

After getting kicked outta the Kahala Towers it seemed like it was all but a matter of time before our time in paradise was over. We bounced around another couple of motels and I got back in my T.V. watching routine again which was kinda nice cause the motels had color. I think Mom was starting to run low on money or something cause we started eating only breakfast and dinner. We managed to sneak into another one bedroomer in Hawaii-kai, illegally of course. But it wasn't gonna last. I re-tried school but it took but a few weeks after Mom said, "pack your bags again," and say aloha to Hawaii.

"You just got here," my teacher Mrs. Kanoa said.

"I know," I said, "we don't stay no place for long."

With that she began to cry.

"Whatta crying about?" I said, "you barely know me."

That kinda made her wail even louder. Adults are crazy I tell you.

Well I'd been crying too if I knew what we was trading paradise for. We landed in Inglewood, California which was nothing more than a giant parking lot with airplanes flying all day and night on top. We stayed about a half a mile off LAX. They call it X "cause the control tower shaped like an X" Rowena said. I'd never seen so many black people living in one place before, not even in the Bronx. I'd wonder why they'd all gotta live in one spot. Wouldn't it be smarter to kinda spread out a little for some elbowroom?

As far as I can tell black folks like to fire off their guns all night long cause that's what we heard just about every night. Our neighbors at the motel sure like to pound the walls and shout at the top of their lungs like someone's getting strangled or sumthin. Mom won't even let us outta the room but I don't know what the big huey is about. It's tough to stay in the room all day cause there's no window in the place except for the little thing at the top of the bathroom. There's T.V. but even that's getting kinda old without being able to run around outside. I think all this darkness is driving me a little nutso after being in Hawaii.

Well, pretty soon after we heard our neighbors pounding on the wood paneled walls we get up the gusto to start pounding them right back and scream at the top of our lungs for them to shut up.

They'd yell back "fuck you, you little fucking chinks!"

We'd yell back "fuck yourself ya fucking drug addicts!"

And so it'd go back and forth a couple a times till they'd shut up. I guess it never occurred to us that they'd just come over and shoot us but we was sick to death of being cooped up. It wasn't long before we was screaming at the top of our lungs at each other and cussing up a storm so they'd have ta pound on the walls and tell us to shut up. That was a twist.

I learned a whole new vocabulary in Inglewood. Meanwhile I can hear Mom screaming at her little sister Hsiu Ying on the pay phone outside.

"Do you know where the heck my children are? That's yet, that's yet!" she'd scream.

"It's where the hell Mom!, not heck," Rowena would say, "It's that's it, that's it, not that's yet," she added. We all started to giggle.

"You…,youuu kids, you think you're Mom can't say fuck! Fucka you kids too." Wow, that's enough to get us all rolling all over the beds laughing so hard our neighbors tell us to "shut the fuck up!"

"Fuck you too!" we say.

Mom eventually gave up on trying to wear out Hsiu Ying on the phone and decided to try a more proven method of fund raising by buying us tickets with the last of our money to Vancouver, B.C. I guess we were going to visit Auntie whether she wanted us to or not. So after about two months, I had my baby blue suitcase all packed and ready and we kicked the doors and pounded the windows of our neighbors before we ran away. It was the middle of the morning so I wasn't surprised that we didn't get a response.

I was surprised to see Auntie Hsiu Ying at the Vancouver airport to pick us up. She had her own blue car called a Nova! It was the nicest car I'd ever seen. Auntie Hsiu Ying was a beautiful lady with wild wavy black hair and perky, pointy tits. She was a lot nicer in person than she sounded on the phone. She was taller and skinnier than Mom and I thought she kinda looked like an auto model.

Vancouver B.C. is the cleanest city I have ever seen in the world. I can't believe how different it is from Inglewood. Vancouver is even cleaner than Honolulu and I guess that makes the Canadians the only people I can think of who have cleaner cities than Americans. Auntie Hsiu Ying even had her own house, which she calls a "bungalow." It's a one-story house with creaky, cold wood floors and wood sided walls and it looks like all the others on the block. She has a son about my age and a daughter about Rowena's age whose names I've forgotten. Maybe I forgot cause we was jealous of all the stuff they had. They were kinda innocent lambs compared to us travelling monkeys.

I guess we were all kinda surprised at how nice Auntie was treating us, feeding us and all, and showing us all around town to the fancy department stores getting ready for Christmas but we soon discovered why we were so useful.

You woulda think that I'd been used to be tossed outta bed in the middle of the night for all kinds of reasons but I just hate getting torn outta a warm pair of sheets. I think I was sleeping standing up for the first half and hour that he was there. I guess Auntie Hsiu Ying was kinda in a fight with her Korean husband who she kicked out. Now they're arguing about who was gonna get the house and other stuff. Auntie ripped us all outta bed and stood us up like a picket fence in between her and her ex who was sitting across the room with a beer in his hand.

I just kind of stood there half dazed with my hair all sticking up in my underwear and I couldn't figure out what the hell we was doing. We just stood there and stood there until my Mom said, "I like your jacket," to Hsiu Ying's husband and he said "it's leather," and then nobody said nothing again for a long time. He just sat there and stared at Hsiu Ying like with the same kinda look that I get when I see a Sicilian style pizza.

I guess he got tired of glaring at and her and not being able to take a bite outta her cause after a little while longer he gets up and throws his beer on the floor cussing and leaves. Well Hsiu Ying starts a whining and crying in front of everyone and I just can't believe she isn't as happy as me that we can all go back to bed again.

It'd been okay if it was just that once that he'd come over but he kept coming back as drunk as a skunk sometimes and there we would be all lined up again like soccer players in front of a penalty kick. Canadian soccer, which they call football, sure is boring. They're T.V.'s kinda like ours except it sucks too. Man, I sure miss our good old American motel T.V.

Well, Rup said, "he'd rape her if we weren't here," so I guess it's a good thing we're here. Sometimes he'd come back twice in a night so we'd have to do our line up all over again. It was getting kinda ridiculous and then one night Rup kinda got tired of standing around and said "why the fuck don't you just go get a prostitute?"

Well Rup had a way of getting under old people's skin and you shoulda seen how hopping mad that Korean got. He just starts slamming his fists through the walls, which are hollow by the way. I was kinda surprised that anyone would buy a house with hollow walls? Anyway he makes his way into the kitchen and just tears the place down before he stampedes outta the house. Maybe he figured he'd bust up the place so bad that she could have it.

It's a good thing Rup is always wise mouthing old people cause they usually don't come back for more. After then he didn't come around anymore. Well we found out at Christmas that Auntie Hsiu Ying wasn't exactly rolling around in dough herself. She had a job as a secretary for a fish packing company so most of our gifts were fish related stuff. That was okay by me cause we could eat it. I never knew there were so many ways to cook a salmon. Mom couldn't give us nothing, which was fine cause we weren't expecting nothing.

But come the day after she broke us the bad news. She said, "don't worry, I'll come get you in a month or two." Rowena and I were wise enough on Mom to know what that meant. Mom's plan was to move all the way back to New York. She said that had been her "plan all along." It was fine with us. The Bronx was just about the only place that I had spent more than a year and half of my life and we all felt a tie to it like no other. It was where I was born, where the Yankees and the Giants play.

So Mom set out with Rup and Carolyn leaving Rowena and me with Auntie and I had this feeling in the pit of my stomach that we might never be Americans again. The longer we stayed in Canada, the more I hated it. All it does is rain and rain and rain in Vancouver. Auntie was nice enough but you could tell she was getting tired of us as well. Her kids kept asking her, "why don't they have to go to school?"

"We're fricken orphans that's why," Rowena would say.

"Don't talk to my children that way!" Auntie would say so Rowena and I would go sit up on the roof where no one could find us.

Rowena and I watched the tall wooden ships sail into the harbor at New York for the bicentennial celebration and I couldn't help but feel proud to be an American. We're way better than these stupid Canadians. The kids that play around this neighborhood are dumb as rocks and we can tell them just about anything and they'll believe us.

Summer eventually came which was good cause it finally stopped raining for a day or two and Auntie took us to some lake, which scared the piss out of me. I'd never seen such huge trees, huge birds and such a wild looking deep lake before. I think I'm kinda afraid of nature. It kinda reminded me of the Land of the Lost. It was so dark in the forest and I felt like we were gonna get attacked by a bear or lion or something. No sir give me New York any day where you know what each street is gonna look like and there are plenty of signs to tell you what's going on. I don't wanna see any trees that are as big as a buildings no more.

Well it wasn't long before it started to rain again and Rowena said, "she's crazy, she's left us."

"No she hasn't," I'd say.

Rowena was starting to talk about running away, about hitchhiking across America. I wasn't so crazy about the idea of running away to anywhere again so I was sure relieved when Mom finally called in August, eight months later.

She sounded like we'd just seen each other yesterday chit chatting about what she'd eat for lunch and how hot and sticky it was today. It's never hot and sticky in Vancouver.

Finally she got around to given us the good news, "Pack your bags," she said, "you're coming home."

She didn't even need to tell us cause my bags are always packed and I'd been living outta it for a long time now. When I do my laundry I just fold it up right into the case. Mom was in a big hurry now cause she wanted us to start the school year off right. I guess she did some fast-talking and made a deal that if we started the year off right we wouldn't have to be left back a grade or two. It was 1976 and in September I would be starting the fifth grade at the annex to P.S. 24 in the White Hall. Man I was excited to be finally going home!

An American Education-James Yu 1976-1978

I guess it got me thinking about the whole thing when I got the assignment from Ms. Slazinger, which she called *what is an American.* If it wasn't bad enough to have to start the sixth grade at a whole new Junior High School 141 in the Bronx, I now had two weeks to come up with why I felt I was an American. I was gonna have to write it out in 1,000 words double spaced so she could rip it to shreds, and then I'd have to get up in the middle of class and give a speech. I'll probably vomit while I'm up there.

I started to think that it might not be such a good idea to start going on and on about how I'd learned everything from T.V. and how book education was a waste of time. Something told me I'd get a bad grade if I did that.

Well I tell you that I racked my brains from day to night for at least two days but nothing was happening with my Bic pen. The only thing I had done was draw a couple of picture of Jaws and one of the Hulk. Well looking back on it a couple of years later now I probably should have cooked up some story about immigrants or something cause everyone at 141 is one. I guess that one would be hard to make original. It's not like we swam over on some inner tube through bombs seeking freedom either. We got here by 747 and hell I don't have a clue why Mom and Dad left the old country anyway.

All I could remember was how much I wanted to be an American when I was stuck up in that hell hole called Canada. I guess it would be truer to say how badly I wanted to be a New Yorker more than anything. It's the place I'm born and that's about all I can explain about that. It got me thinking how I had cried like a puss when I saw the skyline of the city when we landed from Vancouver.

"Mom, I'm finally home," I said. I don't know why I said that cause I didn't really know anything about New York outside of the five blocks I used to live around.

We took a rush hour D train home from the airport and I guess I started seeing a side of New York I never noticed before. I guess I started seeing how others see us as New Yorkers. Well it wasn't the crowds that bothered me that day or the luggage, cause I had seen worse in Asia but it was two smelly bums that kind of turned me around.

The first bum has a whole bench to himself cause he stinks and no one wants to sit next to him I guess even though folks are getting tossed around like rag dolls on the D. Ratta, tattta, tatta, tatta, it sounds like machine gun fire when the train flies on the tracks. Well everything's going fine until we're about two hundred blocks away from our stop when the bum gets this idea in his head he's gotta be a saint and give up his seat for us.

He says to Mom, "lady look, go ahead, go ahead," and points to the bench.

I tell you Mom never does what I think she's gonna cause she up and turns around on him like he was some sort of flee she could swat away. It's right about now that I kind of noticed everyone watching us even though they'd pretend to look at their feet.

"Lady let you kids sit down!" the bum shouts at Mom's cold, back. I think Mom's hypnotized by the black flashing tunnel or somethin cause she's almost smiling or humming a tune or somethin.

The bum just stands there staring at the back of Mom's head and after a little while he starts grabbing his head like he has a splitting headache. I can see people starting to slide to the other end of the car so Rowena and I grab some seats.

To make things worse at the next stop another bum gets on the train with a four-foot wood model of some kinda colonial battle ship. He decides to join our group. The model even has little people and cannons on it painted so you can see each face. I used to see model kits like that all over toy stores in New York but they were never as big as the one he had.

"This bitch won't sit down," the first bum says to the bum with the battle ship. "This bitch won't sit down!"

The bum with the battle ship and all of us just look at our feet.

Rowena whispers to Mom, "please Mom, just sit down."

"Oh you fucking bitch,… you bitch, I'll,…" the bums says waving his arms around in a fit.

Well I guess all the yelling and screaming kind of scared the other bum cause he takes out a twelve inch ribbed bowie knife strapped around his ankle and he starts sobbing like he lost his mind. The knife kinda gets everyone's attention and even the other bum shuts up. The next think you know, he starts stabbing the model ship ripping it to pieces in front of everyone all the while crying away like a freakin baby. After seeing this, the first bum that had been yelling at my Mom for a hundred blocks jumps off the train at the next stop like if somebody farted or somethin.

I kinda thought we should do the same thing but Mom is just standing there with her back to the whole thing oblivious like. Finally, Rowena grabs Mom and shakes her around cause Rowena's almost as big as Mom by now. We got off at the next stop and waited for another train to come along.

It took me an hour to wash the urine out of my sneakers that night. I suppose this is sort of a round about way to explain why I had such a hard time writing my paper on *what makes me an American.* I guess, I just didn't wanta talk about what makes us American cause we were freaks!

I didn't really want to talk about how Mom used her credit cards to pay the rent, or how she used us on the phone to blackmail Dad into sending more money. Or how she kept a safe deposit box so that Dad could never find us or how we had been kidnapped or how she could never keep a job but loved to give people expensive gifts.

Americans weren't supposed to act like that, at least not on TV. So I guess I kinda thought that maybe we was and maybe we weren't Americans.

I suppose, the only thing I could come up with was that I am an American cause I love everything American even if my family doesn't seem to know any of the rules.

So, I wrote about the only thing I could think of and that was sports. I titled my paper, *I'm an American cause I love to play football and basketball, by James Yu.* Well you never heard such a laugh when I read that aloud in class.

Well after that humiliation I should of made up some immigrant stuff and search for freedom and all that like everyone else wrote. I got a lousy C- too, which was another reason I shoulda made something up.

But you know what I kinda believe in that stuff that I wrote. When I play basketball, coach tells me if I give 110 percent, run faster, jump higher, and play harder than everyone else I'll be a starter and I believe him. You know something else; he's not a liar. Coach's made me captain of the Junior All American sixth grade team and he even says he's thinking of recommending me to the all sectional team. The All American sectional team plays teams from all over the country. I sure like the sound of that *All American.*

That's about the only time I feel All American is when I'm beating up on some other American. They don't call me chink after I give them a whopping. I think that most teachers don't think I'm gonna go far in life but they sure treat me different when I can win at sports. Adults sure are nice when you're on their kids winning team and I've been invited to places I never thought I'd see. Some people have two bathrooms in their house!

I guess that's why I never feel nervous playing in front of a crowd cause I'm at home there. The only time I'm at home is when I'm on a court or a field somewhere far from home.

Some people can't believe it when I tell them I missed most of kindergarten to fourth grade.

They say "you poor deprived child," but that's not the way I see it. I think I've had the greatest life cause I've seen so many places in the world. I think I'm gonna make it in America cause I want to be an American. I'm not sure if Mom or Dad could ever figure out who or what they wanted to be.

One other thing about America is you gotta make a lot of money to be happy here. Life was great when Dad's checks kept coming in but by the beginning of the seventh grade Dad was having a change of heart and Mom still couldn't hold a job. I don't know why he stopped sending money but if he coulda seen what happened maybe he woulda changed his mind.

Within a couple months the super cleared us out of the apartment and we ended up on the street next to our furniture. It's kind of strange but I don't think Mom saw it coming cause we just sat out there the whole day on our couch with the street as our living room with the cars passing by like we were gonna camp here for awhile.

I got to see all my friends pass by like Adam Gittstein, Sebastian, Heath, Anthony, and Adam Glickman. It was kind of a low point to see them all waving at me from across the street afraid to come on over to our party. I suppose I could go on and on about how we dragged what we could carry across town looking for I don't know what, and how the mother of a kid I used to beat on at school ended up seeing us and taking us in for the night, and how we ended up in another dive motel, or waking up with cockroaches in your mouth, but even I'm starting to get bored.

I guess what I'm trying to say is it can happen to anyone, even to some big shot like Mom was always claiming to be. I think she kind of missed the point but I don't blame her. I don't think she ever understood what her place in America was. It was like she was an alien or something.

Southern Pilgrimage-Taiwan 1995

Antiquitus saeculi juventus mundi (Ancient times were the youth of the world)-Francis Bacon

A blood-red Ford Festiva makes an unlikely time machine by any stretch of the imagination, but on the right stretch of pavement I suppose anything is possible? Just as an auger drills into the ground exposing a perfect chronological history of the earth, the East Coastal Highway provides a north-south timeline into Taiwan's past. That would make the blood-red Festiva our drill. For the purpose of this metaphor, the Northern capital of Taiwan, Taipei, is our ground zero, our datum for the surface. The further we travel south on the highway the deeper we penetrate into the history of the island.

If we were to hitch a ride on an auger we would find ourselves into the Cenozoic formations of the crust just about when our Festiva crosses the Tropic of Cancer on its way to the tip of the island at Kenting Beach.

Uncle had said, "go to the Koxinga shrine in Tainan if you want to see your family legacy."

In that case, what would any scientist need if he wants to go poking around the earth augering holes here and there? He needs a drill, and we need a car. Tainan is hundreds of kilometers away and I'm hoping for a sturdy ride to battle Taiwanese traffic.

What we get is a blood-red Festiva. A Festiva is a motorcycle wrapped in tin foil barely stout enough to weather bugs and falling bird excrement. Considering how embarrassingly basic my Mandarin is I suppose I should not complain. Apparently, any fool with a credit card can rent a car in the business friendly north.

To get back to our metaphor, we begin our journey by tiptoeing our way into traffic testing our way like a child at the beach. A merge into an arterial and the whole world seems to be crowding by us toward a hole the size of a dime. Now at the wheel responsible for the lives of two people I finally understand what the phrase *Made In Taiwan* really means.

Modern Taiwan is charging forward, there is no looking back. The north is the future; it is present time Taiwan about a few ticks faster than the speed of light. The recent history, the epidermis of Taiwan has been characterized by one thing and one thing alone, *people power.* Not simply just numbers or quantity of people but the *dynamic quality of people.*

It would be easy to scoff at such a statement but consider the resources that Taiwan had to work with, and then consider the results.

In 1950 economists called the island an economic "basketcase" with no likely future prospects. They cited the imbalance of land-to-population ratio, the absence of natural resources, the small internal capital reserves, the loss of markets in Japan and China, the minority government in transition from China, the sudden influx of 1.5 million refugees that the transition produced, and the specter of invasion from the mainland as proof enough that the future was dark. Yet over a period of three decades, Taiwan registered more years of double-digit growth than any nation in the world. For fifteen years, its growth was double Japan's and triple of the U.S. The island has appeared to have developed against all odds.[49]

As a result, Taiwan has been called the *Asian Economic Miracle.* Taiwan is the only country in the world to have transformed itself from an U.S. aid recipient into a major world donor of funds and foreign investment after U.S. aid ended. It has stockpiled, through sound economic planning, one of the world's largest foreign exchange reserves of over U.S. $100 billion in 1999. In the year 2000 there was virtually no unemployment even in spite of the recent Asian financial crisis. The population enjoys one of the highest annual average incomes in Asia at U.S. $12,009 in 1997.[50]

When referring to the *energetic quality* of the Taiwanese people, in contrast to other societies, it is useful to examine other passions of the island's people. Sport is one such prospect, and baseball is a game especially loved by the Taiwanese. Baseball is a useful area to examine because it illustrates clearly that there is nothing on the surface of Taiwanese apparently unique or special biologically, mentally, or otherwise other than their view of life.

Little League Baseball provides a convenient microcosm to study because it has evolved into an international game much more so than its professional counterpart; although, the later is catching up.

Championship years for Taiwanese Little Leaguers' came in:

1969 (Chinese Taipei-5, Santa Clara, CA-0)
1971 (Tainan-12, Gary, IN-3)
1972 (Chinese Taipei-6, Hammond, IN-3)
1973 (Tainan City-12, Tucson, AZ-0)
1974 (Kao Hsiung-12, Red Bluff, CA-1)
1977 (Li-The-7, El Cajon, CA-2)
1978 (Pin-Kuang-11, Danville, CA-1)
1979 (Pu-Tzu Town-2, Campbell, CA-1)
1980 (Long Kuon-4, Tampa, FL-3)
1981 (Tai-Ping-4, Tampa, FL-2)
1986 (Tainan Park-12, Tucson, AZ-0)
1987 (Hua Lian-21, Irvine, CA-1)
1988 (Tai Ping-10, Pearl City, HI-0)
1990 (San-Hua-9, Shippensburg, PA-0)
1991 (His Nan, Tai Chung-11, Danville, CA-0)
1995 (Shan-Hua-17, Spring, TX-3)

In addition, Taiwanese teams have taken consolation honors in 1982 and 1989. That means Taiwanese Little Leaguers' have been to the championship game 53% of the time since 1967.[51]

Since this whole discussion is to draw a parallel between Taiwan's economic success and its successes in other endeavors on the world stage, let us tie the knot. It should shed some light on the recent history of the island's people.

A yardstick that modern economists' use to rank nations in terms of economic growth is to measure their performance compared to others over three decades. In terms of economic years of growth Taiwan leads the world as stated earlier surpassing even that of the United States.[52] Using the same yardstick, Taiwan is also the *Little League Empire of the world,* vastly surpassing all others. The statistics are not even close.

How large is the disparity? Let us examine the statistics one last time from 1967, prior to which very little baseball was played anywhere but in the U.S. We should not forget that baseball is the great American pastime. The epicenter of Little League Baseball is a small town named Williamsport tucked on the Susquehana River in central Pennsylvania, but back to the statistics.

Since 1967 championship years came for six countries of which the breakdown is:

Mexico = 1 Championship
Japan = 4 Championships
South Korea = 2 Championships
Venezuela = 2 Championships
United States = 9 Championships

Those are surprising results when you consider that there is not a single Taiwanese born player in Major League Baseball today. I do not think it is due to a lack of aptitude on the part of the Taiwanese that this is the case.

To drive the point home, once again, an inspection of Taiwan's physical gifts in 1950 could not have forecasted such astronomical successes such that the Taiwanese have enjoyed. There is only one explanation for the results that of the tireless energy of its people and a strong central government committed to unleashing its force. Taiwan, through history and circumstances, has always been a springboard for change. That has been the one constant throughout the history of the island. Change is what the people have become habituated to.

Change is the word for modern Taiwan. Change or be left behind, far, far, far behind.

Now sitting here idling on the surface of the pavement, of Taiwan's history in our Ford Festiva we can clearly see the costs associated with such dramatic change. We drive by pedestrians' scarved in painter's respirators to protect them from air that both sustains and kills in the same breath. It is time we headed south to see where the islands unchanged wilds reside. It is time I found my legacy.

Celestial Highway In the Sky

Those who would hedge or grumble over the need for environmental and land use regulations in America desperately need to live for extended sojourns in Taipei or other developing cities like it. There they could gauge their opinions with every inhalation, the cost for such meteoric development.

Nowhere are the effects of the modern transformations associated with the island's recent success more prevalent than in the bustling cities of the north. For my tender-soft western lungs the dust and smog draped curtain hanging over Taipei is debilitating and as we turn southeast around the northern tip of the island the curtain parts on the gray theater to reveal cool, fresh, Pacific Ocean air.

It is truly stunning to be so rapidly transported from such a degraded environment to one so pristine, natural and relatively clean. The difference is gained in less than 60 minutes. The contrast really does make our Festiva feel like a time machine. The contrast is not lost on the Taiwanese either; as they have grown painfully aware that the spoiling of their island's environment threatens to reverse the quality of life they have labored so dearly to achieve.

Leaving Taipei's moist, humanity infested, traffic weighted ring, in the winter of 1995, marks the beginning of the end of the last leg of my hunt to uncover my roots. The southwestern city of Tainan lies within the cross hairs of our shinning red missile. The urge driving me forward grows more urgent the closer I get. My blood is magnetized with a positive charge and Tainan looms large as the proverbial negative pole. After all, it's been thousands of miles in the making.

Everything relaxes rounding the northern tip. The scenery softens, eyes relax, stomach unclenches, shoulders slump and the grip on the steering wheel rips away like Velcro straps. I cannot say I've ever seen any of this East Coastal region of Taiwan. I think this is what my Dad meant when he said there are "two faces," of Taiwan.

As the road climbs higher into the sky along dark volcanic cliffs, the deep blue endless ocean stretches out like a carpet over our left shoulders. It is a carpet made out of blue light in every shade of the spectrum. In fifth gear we zip past the sleepy coastal community of Keelung, we zoom past Fulung Beach, and slide past Chiao-Hsi.

The East Coastal Highway climbs higher and higher to a dizzying altitude. It climbs so high that we find ourselves in the clouds and the ocean hundreds of meters below. Peaking through the mist are the tan and black eyebrows of the beaches far below.

The difficulty of constructing this highway in the sky is unspeakably epic. To cut a ledge into such hard rock must have required dynamite and endless hours of elbow grease. The cut reveals the Cenozoic past. An hour out of Taipei and we are already treated to the geological monuments that speak of the fiery creation of the landscape. Festiva is a fast acting drill indeed! We can eyewitness the crystalline, thrusted, tilt-fault rock under our tires. The rock tells the prehistory of the land. Tortured curved forms scream of the cataclysmic forces that gave birth to an island. They are incomprehensible forces that bent and snapped rock like twigs.

By noon the early morning mists burns away. Brilliant blue-green glowing landscape replaces the remaining vespers on the embankments. Forests thick with bamboo, the trickling of water flowing down the steep crevices in the cliffs, blue and red high prowled fishing boats sparkling on the ocean, and a crystal clear indigo sky awaken from their slumber.

"This remind me of Big Sur," Lynda says.

It's as if we are riding on opposite sides of the Ring of Fire, a mirror image of Northern California's coastline. Although the geology is similar, the ecology is not.

I'm having an Amy Tan moment. I feel strangely connected to this geography. I have always been drawn to the sea and fishing boats.

Fishing villages are everywhere. The leathered faces of men tending their nets is a scene that could have been replayed thousands of years ago. Some venture into the deep alone on a raft built out of P.V.C. pipes roped together like a pan flute. The rafts are no larger than a four-foot by eight-foot piece of plywood. Like their high prowled cousins, the pipe rafts bend the pipes of the bow skyward to fend off waves and keep from being swamped. This is a common practice in reed boat construction as well. Thousands of years ago fishermen used the same raft design except bamboo was used instead of P.V.C. plastic pipe.

Poly vinyl chloride pipe is a recent invention but it is amazing to see how the basic design of the watercraft has endured right down to the raft proportions. Rafts are typically long and thin so that the pipes or bamboo are long in relation to their width. This allows the material to be bent without snapping and creates an efficient hydrodynamic design for cutting through the water. I have never seen a fat squat raft of this type.

If I blink, I can see myself paddling out on one of these rafts, or am I paddling out on my surfboard back home?

Below the dusting of gray P.V.C. rafts and blue and red fishing boats, lie the leviathan Asiatic and Philippine Sea Crustal plates. They form the boundary of an active subduction zone. A subduction zone is a place where one continental crustal plate bulldozes over another. The whole idea of crustal plates floating as the skin of the earth over a viscous mantle is called plate tectonics. As one slams into another, the earth is folded like a wrinkled throw rug. The cliff highway grows ever higher because of this phenomenon.

Fifty to seventy million years ago we would have needed a submarine to ride on the soil we are on today. At that time, the Philippine Sea Crustal plate east of our current perch on the cliffs rammed over the Asiatic crustal plate to the west while sinking beneath the Ryuku Arc plate toward Japan in the northwest. As massive landmasses met the thrusting and folding of the rock strata on the ocean floor created the island of Taiwan. Taiwan is the wrinkle in the rug. Because the eastern side of the island is closer to the collision it is the side with the steepest cliffs. That is what makes for such precipitously spectacular scenery from our roadway.

Because the force of the collision was primarily east-west, the resulting fold lines were primarily a north-south structure. As a result, the impenetrable mountain ridges created on the island run north-south for 330 kilometers virtually the entire length of the island. The ridges are parallel lines that decrease in height the further west, or furthest from the impact, you go.

West of the five longitudinal mountain ranges the terrain rolls into the smaller fold and thrust belt of the foothills which eventually feather down to the tablelands of the western plains. The plains once again meet the water of the Taiwan Straits. As such, the east is steep and high and the west is flat and tame. A cross section of the island would look approximately like a ramp to the east.

It is not surprising then that the island evolved cultural distinctions from east to west as well as north to south. First off, the mountains create a distinct geographical divide for rivers and water as well as history and culture. The north-south ridges divide the watersheds to east and west. Rivers on the east-side flow down steep gradients and their rapid descent has carved a unique landscape. Rivers to the west start steep in the headwaters but eventually mellow into large lumbering channels ideal for navigation and irrigation.

Farming is ideal on the western plains, while fishing and foraging are more likely on the east. Flat land is ideal for development and large cities. Steep cliffs are not. As a result, the wild natural habitats left on the island are predominantly on the eastern side of the island. The eastern side of the island is rugged and remote. Along with several offshore islands it remains the last bastion of indigenous settlements. These are the places the first people of Taiwan have been pushed to.

The geologic story of Taiwan continues today. Like California, Taiwan is still on the Ring of Fire, a place of crustal plates convergence, and they are currently converging at 7 cm per year. The road we drive on in the sky is reaching ever higher still.

Like its geology, Taiwan has always been characterized by *change*. It is quite literally a meeting place for it right down to the earth. Also, like its geological alterations, the changes to the island have often come quite dramatically and destructively. The island has been a host to wave after wave of human migrations and struggles for cultural supremacy.

Conversely, as evidenced by the Chi-Chi earthquake on September 21, 1999 that killed 2,400 people and injured 10,000 more, the island is far from an end to geologic teraforming surprises from below. Chi-Chi alone amassed 20 to 30 billion U.S. dollars in damages.[53]

We stopped on our first night in Hwalien. Hwalien is a vibrant East Coastal town full of local flavor, small crowded seafood restaurants, and cozy hotels. Located approximately one-third down the island it is the perfect springboard to our next destination the Taroko Gorge National Park. If there is one place in Taiwan you cannot miss on a visit, Taroko Gorge is it.

The reason is because it is one of the few places on the island which has remained *un-changed*. By un-changed I should rather say un-touched by the recent dynamism of man. It is a place where one can fully measure just how much Taiwan has altered from its wild and rugged ecological roots. The entire natural history of the island is stored in its high cliffs and deeply incised valleys. The gleaming marble mountains are the very tombs of the primordial ocean's dead inhabitants. They were to be cooked in the kiln of the earth itself to later rise out of the ashes into the sky powered by a tectonic elevator. The marble mountains are created literally from eons of dead sea life.

If you can picture 500 meter tall ceramic pots then you can start to see what these cliffs are. Of course Taroko Gorge was not a gorge at all in the beginning. It was only after millions and millions of years of rain and wind erosion that the near vertical cuts in the rock layers were formed. What makes Taroko unique is the shear verticality and narrowness of the canyons. Cut from stout, hard, abrasion resistant rock, the polished landforms are like no other that I have ever seen. Taroko is like a sharply cut gleaming diamond as opposed to a crumpled clay pot with broadly beveled edges for canyon walls. The funny thing about it is Lynn and I had never heard of the Taroko Gorge, yet it is one of earth's great wonders without a doubt. It is wonderful to know that you don't need a time machine to visit a land before time; you just need to visit Taroko Gorge by car.

This brings me to the main point of coming to Taiwan in the first place that of answering the question "does Ilha Formosa still exist physically or only in the mind?"

It does indeed! The wild places in Taiwan are as beautiful now as the day Jan Huygen Van Linschoten landed proclaiming the place "beautiful island."

The wilds are not confined merely to the Gorge boundaries either. There are over 400 species of birds, over 400 species of wild butterflies, as many as 2,500 species of shelled mollusks, and a dizzying array of insects and invertebrates *still living* on this heavily developed island. There is a very visible tug of war going on still. Who thinks of Taiwan as a safari destination? Perhaps, if the wilds of Taiwan are to be preserved the word needs to get out.

To appreciate just how much unique endemic life remains to be maintained on the island some comparison are useful. For instance, the island of Britain has only 61 species of butterflies compared with the over 400 that inhabit the breezes of Taiwan. Britain has a land area seven times greater than Taiwan.[54] Biologist Lu Kuang-yang states "there are still many unrecorded invertebrates in Taiwan's mountain areas, without a doubt, we don't even have names for them."

Kwan-Tsao Shao, a research fellow at Academia Sinica's Institute of Zoology notes that since the publication two years ago by marine biologists of a *Catalogue of Taiwan's Fish Species*, over one-hundred new fish species have been found along the coast.[55]

I don't think anyone, outside of a few scientists, thinks of Taiwan as a biological and ecological gem along the lines of say Hawaii or the Galapagos. Yet the astounding endemic variety and biodiversity of the island flora and fauna warrant such comparisons. The diversity is attributed to the tropical, sub-tropical and alpine climatic variations that are found at times within miles of each other.

Like many plants and animals of Hawaii, many species on Taiwan are only found on Taiwan. For instance, of the 2,500 species of shelled mollusks, 60-70 percent of the islands land snails are endemic.[56] That means when these species are wiped out, they will be wiped clean from the face of the earth as well. As Taiwanese zoologist Dr. Wu Hai-yin expresses so poignantly, "the plants and animals have always been there; we're just recording them before they die out."[57]

In fact, there is so much biological diversity and unidentified flora and fauna on land and sea that biologists are not consoled by the mundane discoveries of new species! It serves only to remind them their discoveries will not keep pace with the extinction of many animals like the Formosan spotted leopard.

To change or to *un-change,* and how fast to do it? Those are the questions facing tomorrow's Taiwan. *Perhaps, the greatest challenge to the well being of the Taiwanese is not invading communists but the internal destruction of Ilha Formosa from unchecked growth.*

Two-thirds down the island I realize that I really was the banana that Dad said. Everything that I had learned or thought I knew about Taiwan was superficial up to that point. I don't know why I never pictured Taiwan as a maturely evolved society with all the advances, retreats, aspirations and problems of our own society. I really only knew the Amerocentric side of myself and of Taiwan as well. I really only knew one side of Taiwan. I knew the surface, the gossamer skin that had been the past 40 years and I really didn't even understand that. I never bothered or wanted to look beneath before now. Taiwan is not just *Made In Taiwan*, a label. It is a complete and full world unto itself.

Taiwan will need to solve Taiwan's problems with the same ingenuity it has exhibited in the past. Of course, that does not mean they will not need help, but the people of Taiwan seem well versed to the needs of their society. They are well aware of the need to balance issues of growth, quality of life, and economic stability. Taiwanese make up one of the most literate constituencies in the world and the result has been a society with a healthy dose of competing interests vying for the good. Taiwan has evolved into one of the world's most healthy democracies, a place of old and new striving to live in harmony.

To show how surprisingly progressive Taiwan's people are we should examine today's political landscape. Decades of marshal law under the KMT did not change the values and desires of the people for representation. At, virtually the first opportunity to vote the KMT out of power they exercised their opinions by voting in the minority pro-independence Green party in the 2000 election. They elected Chen Shui-bian president even as Beijing threatened war if pro-independence became a policy of the government. It was only the second free election on the island since the lifting of marshal law. But changes do not happen overnight and Chen's halting of the construction of the island's fourth nuclear power plant almost got him recalled. Just days into his term the president was already fighting for his political life. Years of what the Taiwanese call "black gold" politics cannot be reversed in days. "Black gold" politics along with maintaining peace across the Taiwan Strait remain the greatest challenges for the government and people of Taiwan.[58]

Having finally reached land's end at the most southern point of the island at Kenting Beach after days in the car we are rewarded with an amazing 270 degree panorama of the South China Sea. It is a razor sharp clear day, and standing under an acacia tree I can see the Philippines, the south China coast, miles of blue water and a nuclear power plant a stone throw away. That sums up my journey and impressions of the island. Will it be *change at all costs* or will the breaks of *un-changing* be applied. The competing values are written everywhere on the landscape.

One thing is for certain no matter who is in control of the island. Ilha Formosa still lives and it is worth saving not just for Taiwanese but especially for them. The problems for Taiwan are much like those we face in America except everything is concentrated, and distilled more powerfully because of the high people to land ratio. Pollution is more in your face, traffic is more in your face, and natural beauty shines brighter because it is so unexpected when it hits you from just around the corner.

Those at the helm of Taiwan are faced with unbelievable challenges ahead no matter who they are. Will the legacy of Taiwan be the humpback fish that have appeared around Taiwan's nuclear power plants? Biologists flippantly state they are not a stable "new species," and they will not be placed on the list for endangered protection.[59] Or will the legacy of Taiwan be the growing number of Cultural Heritage Preservation Laws, National Parks Laws, and Wildlife Conservation Laws that have saved immense tracks of virgin ecosystems already? Public outcries that drafted laws resulted in 67 established areas protecting native flora and fauna, six National Parks, eighteen nature reserves, 24 natural forest reserves, twelve coastal reserves, and seven wildlife refuges.[60] Or will Taiwan be invaded and placed under the considerations and priorities of Beijing?

The amazingly dynamic tug of war will continue on for many years and who can say how the island will evolve? What is encouraging is that Taiwan remains a leader in Asia for progressive proactive thought. For instance, the Executive Yuan's Commission on Sustainable Development recently stated "Taiwan's flora and fauna are the basis of its sustainable productive forces. Regardless of how resources are used, we must guarantee that their ecological integrity and diversity are preserved. If habitats are brought into conflict with economic development, the protection of natural habitats should take precedence."[61] Wow! We may have yet to see the golden age of Taiwan. If past performance is any indicator of future successes, my money is on the Taiwanese.

Ancestor Worship, Koxinga Shrine-1995

All women become like their mothers. That is their tragedy. No man does. That is his.

Oscar Wilde, *The Importance of Being Earnest*

It is not often that one is given the opportunity to look into the eyes of a four hundred-year-old ancestor-especially not one that is a supposed living god. I guess it is like the unquenchable thirst that drives orphans to seek out their biological parents. To just learn a little more about yourself is a powerful motivation. Our drive up the new super freeway along the western plains is only hours compared to the days we idled winding down the old East Coast route. It's sad to be on such a modern pace.

As we move north our battle tested Festiva propels us back into the present, but not before we make one more stop. It is the most important. From Kenting Beach, we are into Tainan City, the ancient capital of Taiwan, within the blink of an hour. To arrive at my pilgrimage site we must pass through the port city of Kaohsiung, and I can only describe it as the most polluted place on earth. To inhale is a foul, caustic experience and a cloud hangs over the city even on the clearest day at the coast a few meters away. The "two faces" of Taiwan is never far away. To get to the most culturally progressive city in Taiwan we have to pass through its most polluted. It seems only appropriate for an island harboring many extremes.

The geometry of my search has wound full circle to the place of my ancient origins. I recall only dirt roads and low buildings of a sleepy town in 1974. Naturally, Tainan has stirred since then. Tainan is now Taiwan's fourth largest city with a population in excess of 700,000. However, it has managed to retain a measure of the ambiance of the ancient country charm of old. As Taiwan's oldest modern city it has a historical flavor unlike its modern counterparts such as Taipei. Tainan is to Taiwan what Kyoto is to Japan and Kyongju is to Korea. It is the birthplace of my bloodline, the genetic womb of my mother.

Tainan, the city that Koxinga built, remains the most culturally endowed as well as the most persistent sentinel of traditional practices on Taiwan. It is a city of temples and shrines. The roads are laced in an ancient pattern with a maze of narrow lanes, courtyards and garden walls tucked into a landscape from the Imperial past. Most residents speak the native Taiwanese dialect. They often use it instead of Mandarin Chinese. Indigenous religious festivals such as the pai-pai are still an integral part of the rhythm of people's lives. Judging from the number of trucks, cars, and scooters lurching about, I would not describe their lives as slow paced but by Little League Empire standards it is molasses.

My pilgrimage to the Koxinga Shrine delivers us to the very heart of the old downtown. As I near the gates to the shrine I am charged with an electric sense of anticipation. I can only think of one thing to do first. I need to find the statue of Koxinga so that I can see what it is that I am born from.

Lynn says, "go ahead, then." She sees my impatient energy.

I can't even control my legs and they are soon running in a most undignified pace. I leave her in the dust of the great stone quadrangle in front of the museum. What I came to do I guess is best done alone.

The Koxinga shrine was built in 1875 by imperial edict from the Manchu court in Beijing. The same court that murdered Koxinga's parents had appointed the commission. The Manchu now feigned the white flag of reconciliation signaling that the former Ming resistance leader was forgiven and to be deified as a national hero. The Japanese occupation left the shrine in ruins until it was restored after the war and then once again in 1962. Major memorial festivities for the father of modern Taiwan are held three times a year-on February 12 (the date of the Dutch surrender to Koxinga), April 29 (retrocession day) and August 27 (Koxinga's birthday). I am searching for the statue of Koxinga that stands in the central shrine hall flanked by his two most trusted generals. It is not as easy to find as you would think.

I'm ashamed to say I hardly notice the Fuchou-style temples that flank the gardens at the time. They are supposedly the only ones in Taiwan. I stumble through an interpretive center and museum displaying antiques, pottery, paintings, documents and costumes but that can wait till later. I rumble by the rear shrine hall housing an altar to Koxinga's mother but no husband. I only stop for a moment to pay my respects.

By the time I emerge from the altar I'm sweating profusely. The altar exit dumps me into the middle of a huge garden. At least it is cooler in the grounds. This compound was certainly not laid out by a Cartesian trained Quaker. There is not one ninety degree in the whole place. I'm lost, plain and simple. Lost inside the Koxinga shrine.

I'm too embarrassed now to stop running. So I manage to run myself all the way to the end of the grounds until I can't run anymore because there is a wall there. I can hear the rumbling of street cars and fruit vendors selling star fruit and dried plums on the other side. This is good because at least I know where I am now, at the end. I keep following along the wall east until "viola," I'm back where I started at the entrance gate. Thirty minutes have passed.

Time for lap number two. A few minutes later, I'm relieved to see Lynn standing by an interpretive center display.

Lynn says, "did you go for a jog?"

"Haa, haa, haa, haaa," I say.

"The statue is quite green," she says.

"Where is it?"

She hands me the museum guide that shows exactly where it is with a big black X.

I think the thing I noticed the most was how quiet it was inside the compound compared to the outside world. The only thing I hear are my footsteps on the limestone floor lining the colonnade to the shrine.

The shrine is set inside a grand earth colored stucco temple with dragon arched green and blue tiled gable roofs. The immaculately white limestone path is a wonderful contrast. They lead me to the feet of the recumbent statue.

Lynn's arm slips away.

"Incredible," I whisper.

I'll be dammed, Confucius was right all along.

Here I am after thousands of miles, years of thought, and painful reflection. I'm looking into the eyes of a Taiwanese legend, a god. *Koxinga is deified* in a statue of the man seated in a traditional green full-length Mandarin gown. He sits gazing at the world in an Abraham Lincoln Memorial statue pose. His left hand grasps at his belt on the waist and his right hand is clenched in a fist resting on his thigh. Each gesture signals an ancient sign language of imperial authority.

This is the history that I rejected as irrelevant in my birth home America. But now that I am here I do not cry. In fact, I'm not choked up at all?

After awhile I pass through a moon door and rejoin Lynn.

"Did you have your Amy Tan moment," she said?

"Yes," I said, "yes I did," but what I was thinking was no, no I didn't.

"Remember that time I visited you in D.C. and you took me to the Lincoln Memorial?" I said to Lynn.

"Memorial Day weekend," Lynn said. "We went to the Mall to see the fireworks and music."

"Yeah, that's it," I said. "That's kind of how I thought I was going to feel. A little bit tingly."

But that's not what happened. I had no melancholy tingling, no holding back the tears. It was years later that I knew why.

Confucius had said that for the kings of ancient China to create a society of law-abiding subjects they must attend to the rituals of state.

They must not be derelict in their yearly ceremonies, they must not ever allow the illiterate masses to stray from the idea of the nation under the imperial authority of heaven itself. It's too late for me to be anything other than American.

Confucius knew that there is something from your childhood that you can never fully unlearn. He warned the kings as such. You have to have the right propaganda to rule. People have to feel like they are part of something that they like. That is the impossibly powerful draw of China and America as well. After years of the pledge of allegiance and so on and so forth I was never going to have an Amy Tan moment, at least not in Taiwan.

I could not have guessed that by traveling half way around the world, seeing natural wonders beyond compare, and finally worshipping at the feet of a four-hundred year old ancestor deified as a god that *I would suddenly feel homesick.*

By coming to the Koxinga shrine and Taiwan, I did find my home but it was not in Taiwan. My Amy Tan moment did not happen in Taiwan but what it revealed was my American-ness. Although I gazed into the face of Koxinga I could not get past the image of my mother in his eyes. I know my mother to be far short of god-like qualities and I cannot accept Koxinga as anything more than a man. I have no doubt that he was any extraordinary man but he is only great, great, great, great, great grandpa to me.

I don't want to seem unimpressed or offend those who worship him. I was impressed. For those who grew up with his legend and the rituals and rhythms of life associated with it there is more. I only know that when I hear the 1812 overture played on the mall on the Fourth of July, I shed a tear. I have been programmed just like Confucius knew I would be. I was programmed willingly. Dad was right all the time I am a banana. I am an American through and through and I think that must mean an American is that which was never before.

By traveling to Taiwan for the third time I confirmed for all time that my home is America. I was born in America and it will always be my home. *Home is where your future lies no matter what obstacles or prejudices lie there.* The day that there is no future in

America for my family or me is the day I may have to search for a new home. But I cannot see that day coming anytime soon.

At the Koxinga shrine ancient rock forms and bamboo line a pond and listen appreciatively to the sound of water moving over them. That day I found the source of my mother's legendary pride, which she attempted to instill in me. With all this to one lone man how could she not have seen the world as she did? The shrine and works of our ancestor are grandly depicted and they do take on god like proportions.

My feelings of shame of my ethnic heritage, or feelings of backwardness for being Asian are long gone now. I know we all must come from somewhere. Some even have to bear the burden of being derived from a god. I guess I shouldn't complain.

The Dao in ancient times was in China but today it is in America because America today at least attempts to address the eternal societal injustices. The convergence of 5,000-year-old Chinese philosophy and of the Constitution is ironic indeed. In Confucius day the same problems persisted as today and his teaching sought merely to create a governmental system of moral and just order. When asked by Baron K'ang Ch'i about the role of government in life, Confucius replied, "Government is merely setting things right. When you yourself lead them by right example, who dares to go astray?"[62] Ancient China thrived under Confucius's teaching but the communists today share less in their enthusiasm of his legacy as they did in the past.

America on the other hand today attempts to accommodate those from all parts of the world along with their new ideas, which may actually be old ideas from somewhere else. America is not perfect of course and falls short all the time but the eternal truth remains. You cannot maintain strength by closing off ideas new or old from unwanted sources. The natural selection of ideas must take its own course. Confucius knew this as well. When asked by the Duke of Yeh about good government he said, "Good government consists in winning the loyalty of the people nearby and attracting the people far away." He adds, "When the ruler shows kindness to the strangers from far countries, people from all quarters of the world will flock to the country." As far as I can tell, there is very little rush of immigrants except starving North Koreans eager to relocate to China today. On the other hand busses and boats full of illegal refugees continue to stream into America. What is the reason for this? The Dao is in America today. China is relearning the Dao, which came from it in the first place.

It is interesting to note that the teachings of Confucius, which are thousands of years old, are as relevant today as they ever were. Of course there are elements which taken out of context mean very little to modern society today but it is the attempt to answer the eternal question of morality and justice that have rendered them timeless. Consider the following passage, "For every one called to the government of nations and empires there are nine cardinal direction to be attended to:

1. Cultivating his personal conduct.
2. Honoring worthy men.
3. Cherishing affection for, and doing his duty toward, his kindred.
4. Showing respect to the high ministers of state.
5. Identifying himself with the interests and welfare of the whole body of public officers.
6. Showing himself as a father to the common people.
7. Encouraging the introduction of all useful arts.
8. Showing tenderness to strangers from far countries.
9. Taking interest in the welfare of the princes of the Empire.

Consider also the principle of reciprocity or *shu*, which is a Chinese equivalent to the Golden Rule. The translation comes out backwards, which isn't surprising but the meaning is the same. "Look into yourself and do not do something you would not have pleasure with another doing to you."[63]

Although, I did not see many timeless truths reflecting on the face of my ancestor I did see them written on the walls of the Taroko Gorge and other wild areas of Taiwan. Ilha Formosa will always have a place in my heart but it is not my home. My home is in America, where the Dao of my life lives.

Wetlands and High Tech Fabs
Hillsboro, OR 2001

One hundred twenty-five years ago when Hillsboro, Oregon was incorporated, little more than Atfalati Indians lived in this area of the Tualatin River Valley. It is ironic that the face of the first Oregonian is the face of the forgotten Asian tribes. The valley located twelve miles west of the then frontier town of Portland was known as the East Tualatin Plains prior to incorporation. The Tualatin River winding through this flat plain was named after the Indian word "twality" which some say means "lazy river." Of course, everything changed when Hillsboro was incorporated in 1876. By then, the area had been renamed after the pioneer David Hill who crossed over the Rocky Mountains in a wagon train into what was then the Oregon Territory. Ever since then, the face of an Asian in Hillsboro has been the face of a stranger, a foreigner or recent immigrant.

Sometimes, I wonder what Bill and Mary Smith, the Mormons who live next door, might feel if they knew their neighbor were descended from notorious Asian pirates. Pirates who lay siege, killed, and crushed a white Christian army four hundred years ago. I wonder because our relationship is such that I have no intention of telling them, at least not directly. I'm not sure they would even believe that the engineer next door could be derived from a man who commanded

100,000 swarthy brown warriors. Yet here I am finally arrived in American suburbia, an Asian face returned to the valley. I am a newcomer. That is the beauty today of Hillsboro, Oregon. It is so new that just about anyone in the world could move in next door. The modern society that we all enjoy today naturally had a price tag that was paid dearly by the Indians that no longer live here.

Swaty an Indian Hindu woman and her husband Sebastian from France lives a few houses south of ours with their two daughters. Across the street from them are Indonesian Buddhists who purified their house in a red and yellow robed ritual before they moved in. A whole congregation of Mormons and their even larger herd of children surround us. A block away, Mannie and his wife who love to play golf live with their half Mexican and Philippino daughter. Across the street from them, Chris, Mike, their son and an adopted Negro daughter live. A few doors up a mulatto boy Isaac plays outside his driveway. There is amazing diversity in our little new 100-lot subdivision. The world lives here.

For the most part we have arrived via the mother ship of high technology and high tech apparel manufacturing. Just about every family is either employed at the Intel fab or another of the new tech campuses that litter Washington County the seat of Hillsboro. The County has been dubbed the Silicon Forest. Those who are not high tech workers might punch the time clock over at the Nike world campus or man a drill press over at the Columbia Sportswear world headquarters, or labor at another of the businesses built out of the modern economy. The Nike Campus, which would put most college campus to shame both in size and facilities, is a shinning example of the new industries that just did not exist a generation ago. Washington County is about the future. What ten years ago were two lane dirt roads through miles of virgin forest or fields are now four lane paved highways lined by endless subdivisions and commercial parks.

There are few places in history that have developed with the alacrity of Hillsboro, Oregon. It is a place that has attracted the best and the brightest from all over the world as a result of its information intensive technology based industries. It is an ultra dynamic place that is full of life, where the Dao of living is today. It is a thoroughly American place. Hillsboro, Oregon is the future face of America, a multi-ethnic taco salad. The can do optimism is a result of the post-Brady Bunch, post cell phone baby boom energy in each of its young inhabitants. The average age of a person in Hillsboro grows younger with each passing census. Anything seems possible but with those possibilities come many interesting questions. One is how will sense be made out of all of the crazy diversity, the kind of which may have existed only in small urban pockets of New York City or Los Angeles.

Our neighbor's kids are part Indian, French, Italian, English, Irish, Chinese, Japanese, African, Russian, Mexican, Vietnamese, Korean and many others. They are not individual pockets of Italians, or Irish but a true mixture of many races all in one family. I wonder how they are going to define themselves within the American landscape when there has been for recent memory one unifying white constant, and will they have a sense of what it cost to get there? It may be that they will have to rewrite a new history of their own. It is all in the hands of Eli and his multi-hued contemporaries. They all get along so wonderfully, so easily, as children.

I also wonder if they will realize that everything in Hillsboro, Oregon is imported and foreign? Will they understand that maple trees lined along the right of way do not grow naturally at 25' on center and that water does not naturally disappear and evaporate from the streets or will it all be taken for granted as having always been here? Everything in Hillsboro today is a reflection of merely over 100 years of American values but you could never guess of it by driving the streets today. In such a dynamic environment, those values are evolving as I type out these words and I cannot imagine how the world will differ from the world I knew as mine differed from my fathers. I wonder if Eli's generation will have a greater understanding of their neighbors than I have had? I wonder if they will have a greater understanding of themselves than I have had?

It will be exciting to see how the social experiment of Hillsboro turns out. It will be a reflection on the future of the world in a sense because the world now lives here. How it turns out may be molded in part by how we are able to get along in the present. Our futures may lie in our ability to understand each other and ourselves in a way we have never before been able to. Do most of us know even the simplest questions of where we come from or where we are going with a great deal of depth? I can say with honesty that I did not.

In 2001 the Dali Lama, the exiled spiritual leader of the Tibetan Buddhists visited Portland, OR. In his speech at Pioneer Square in downtown Portland, he announced to throngs of thousands of Oregonians that he felt that the human race appeared to be evolving into a more mature state of awareness and that peace in the world was a result of it. I sincerely hope so. I have my doubts because the greatest and most painful coming of age lesson I learned by my trip into the past was the realization that no matter how much logic, rational, or discussion there is, there are still some things that can not be reconciled even between father and son much less society. I will never see the world like my father sees the world. I have resigned to accept it is just impossible and in a way it has helped me accept others who are just plain different from me. My father's and my experiences in life are just too far apart.

How will the Taiwanese people reconcile their differences with the Mainland Chinese? According to President of the communist party, Jiang Zemin, Taiwan's formal status as a part of China will never be up for negotiation. Taiwan and China's experiences are virtual polar opposites and I do not believe within this climate the time for peaceful reconciliation to be ripe. But Jiang Zemin is 75 years old and plans to retire in 2002. The communist party leadership is expected to be in transition in the coming years. For now, an unnatural union at this time in history would seem to be against nature. There is currently very little incentive for Taiwan to reenter the fold of Chinese suzerainty. Perhaps, as with my relationship with my father, time may provide the lubricant for providing solutions to problems that logic, philosophy or laws cannot, after the old, and embittered have waned away on both sides of the straits. Perhaps, as in Jiang Zemin's own words while quoting a Song Dynasty poem:

"People part and meet, they have sorrow and joy, just like the moon that wanes and waxes."

It was never my intent to discredit the Communist Mainland Chinese claims over ownership over the island of Taiwan in my story. After all as I have stated before, I am an American and I do not see myself as qualified to talk on behalf of the Taiwanese or the Chinese people. It is true that I am a Taiwanese American, but I am also a Chinese American too. Somewhere deep down there is Japanese in me as well. I have a love for all the legacies that I am derived. It is a schizophrenic state of self-awareness.

I wrote our family story merely to bring light to a perspective that I myself habitually discounted, the view from behind the eyes of my parents and their contemporaries. Our story is about Taiwanese and Taiwanese Americans and it does not presume to be an unbiased scientific treatise on international law although at times it wanders into that territory by necessity. The events that are occurring on Taiwan today were of no surprise to my family and to Taiwanese. When Uncle Lee, as we called him when I was a toddler, shared the warmth of our radiator on the seventh floor of a Bronx brownstone for Thanksgiving in 1969 the seeds for its transformation were already sowed into its soil. Uncle Lee went on to become President Lee Teng-hui, the first native Taiwanese born leader of the island, but before that he was a lover of turkey breast in cranberry sauce and a struggling Cornell University grad student.

Today's Taiwanese leaders were yesterday's starving scholars in the United States like my father and mother. They were a very small tight knit group of Taiwan's best and brightest sent out to bring back the educational gems of the West. They all knew each other during their heady times of youth and it was not surprising to have them over for social occasions when they were nobodies. My mother was already a celebrity of sort from the Old World so our house was a natural meeting place for Thanksgiving dinners.

What these men and women came away with was more than Master's degrees and PhD's but a taste of freedom and ideals American style. In the past fifty years, Taiwan has been affected by American culture far more than by the stagnant Chinese society that claims to own it. Hillsboro-ism has exerted its irresistible force wherever it has landed. It remains as our most lasting and greatest source of export. It is the promise of a future regardless of your past.

It is interesting to note that in the last two island wide presidential elections that the people of Taiwan have supported strong Independence platform candidates in spite of Chinese threats of invasion. Taiwanese are among the most educated and sophisticated electorates in the world with literacy rates higher than our own. How else could they have voted? Poll after poll of the general population have shown that the meat of the Taiwanese bell curve rebuts Chinese reunification schemes. The people just do not see it in their best interest to do so at this time.

The million-dollar question is, will the people of Taiwan have the luxury to determine their own destiny or will geopolitical giants resolve it for them, and will there be violence involved? There is little doubt that the United States and China are the principal brokers in the fate of the small island.

But beyond the two super powers the future fate of Taiwan is an international issue as well. According to an article in *The Japan Times Online,* "The denial by the PRC of the Taiwanese people's right to freely determine their own future status and the country's exclusion from the U.N, tolerated by big powers, is one of the greatest human-rights abuses of the past century." The article by Alexander K. Young, a professor of international relations, emeritus, at the State University of New York illustrates how the minute Pacific Island state of Tuvalu with only 10,000 inhabitants recently became the 189th member of the U.N., while Taiwan's exclusion remains as "one glaring injustice."[64]

Mr. Young points out that the exclusion is a violation of the U.N.'s very own charter which states in Article 4 that "membership in the U.N. is open to all other peace-loving states (ie., other than the Charter members) which accept the obligations contained in the present Charter, and, in the judgment of the Organization are able and willing to carry out these obligations." He states that as Taiwan is the 14th largest trading country on earth and a nation with one of the world's largest foreign exchange reserves, it should be able to carry out U.N. obligations. For instance, Taiwan extended $300 billion in aid to Kosovo refugees.

On top of U.N. charter violations he states, "it is a violation, above all, of the principle of universal representation. It is also contrary to Article 1 of both the International Covenant on Economic, Social and Cultural Rights and the International Covenant on Civil and Political Rights, according to which "every people has the right of self-determination."[65]

The gap between the argument on the other side of the coin is similar to the chasm that can exist between one generation and the next, Lawrence Welk and MTV. No amount of logic thrown into the argument will suffice to produce an agreement. The Chinese view Taiwan as a part of the Empire of China and that is simply final. There is an emotional component tied to the Chinese argument tied up into the history and pride of what it means to be Chinese, part of an imperial society that has survived perhaps longer than any other on earth. It has nothing to do with self-determination of peoples. It is a vision of a glorious united nation that may someday be the most powerful in the world.

The Chinese argument has its appeal to Chinese everywhere and I am no exception. Chinese everywhere have long viewed themselves as underdog on the world stage and rightfully so. China was treated roughly by many foreign hands. Recently, I met an engineer, a Mr. Cherng, at an engineering conference along the coast of Oregon at Lincoln City. After polite salutations and chitchat, I learned he was originally from Taiwan. His eyes lit-up when I revealed coincidentally that I was a Taiwanese American as well. As our speaker labored on in monotone about building code jargon nuances, we gladly began a conversation on the current political climate on the island of our common descent.

"Yes," I told him, "I've heard that Chen Shui-bian was elected president."

"He is an advocate for independence," Mr. Cherng said in a tone that stressed *I can't believe it!*

"What's wrong with that," I whispered back after a moment?

The question was followed by an awkward silence, which to my disappointment changed the complexion of our cozy little intimate conversation. We sat like strangers next to each other where a few moments before we were thick as thieves.

Eventually, I asked Mr. Chreng when his ancestors had arrived on Taiwan and it confirmed my suspicion. He said his family had arrived with the Chiang Kai-shek nationalist in the wave of immigration from the mainland following World War II.

He seemed to sense what I was thinking because he added, "it's not because I am a mainlander that I do not support independence. I just don't believe there is any *future* for Taiwan in independence." That was the end of our conversation until we said our polite goodbyes. Mr. Chreng's point is not lost on me. I have wondered the same. However, if it were my father I'm sure the two would have quickly advanced from polite conversation to kung fu battle rather shortly. Whether I am entitled to or not, I am open to any ideas that are in the best interest of Taiwan. However, I remain unconvinced that any such ideas should be the result of anything other than the will of the 23 million living on the island. That I believe is a reasonable place to draw the line. Of course, the outcome will be the litmus test of whether we do live in a more mature state of being or not, as the Dali Lama expressed.

The issue of Taiwan presents a unique challenge for the American government and people. Whether American's realize it or not, the government of the United State for better or worse has a legal obligation to ensure the autonomy and security of Taiwan under the 1979 Taiwan Relations Act. It also has the problem of honoring obligations in the region to other countries such as Japan and South Korea in the containment of China and the promotion of open markets and American values. As a result, America is in the unenviable position of riding a fence by trying to develop relations with the Chinese giant and encouraging it to evolve in a friendly way, while honoring its commitments to the satellites around it. It has resulted in the Bush administration's thinking to disengage in Europe and shore up resources in the Pacific. The Pacific Theater is the future of the world.

The most precious commodity in preserving peace in the region may be none other than time. It will take time for the internal structure of the Communist machine to evolve into a modern consumer based economy and for old ideas to be replaced with new without chaos erupting in China. There still exists too wide a gap in understanding and interpretations of world history even within China's borders. When the new world order arrives, China may be just happy to retain its current configuration and forget about little islands offshore. What has occurred in Russia could easily erupt in China.

Oddly enough, we are faced with the same problems at home in the states as the face of our own nation transforms. To keep the peace at home we will be forced to learn and appreciate more about the strange neighbors we see growing around us. Perhaps, the new lessons we learn in dealing with the world in our own backyard will be the formulas for solving problems outside the box in places far away. This is my hope at least.

Back in Hillsboro, on the other side of our house from the Mormons, two women share the house to the east, and we can clearly see they are a lesbian couple. They are nice people who like to carol their neighbors during Christmas. They are both elementary school teachers and are fine neighbors. We get along with them just fine. To the west a house beyond the Mormons, our subdivision is so new the street dies into goat pasture two houses away. Lynn and I are hoping they never take down the vehicle barrier to develop the next parcel so the basketball hoops can stay up and the kids out. I suspect our illusions of cul-de-sac life are short lived in the fastest growing county of Oregon. We saw the women's house next door rise from the Tualatin Valley clay wondering the whole time "who would move in?"

I never thought that I would be able to afford America but somehow it has worked even for someone with as humble an origin as mine. That is the Dao of the future. But I did not buy my way into America. My future began when I became a father to Eli, and so the story continues.

Epilogue

We live today in relative tranquility in our homes in Hillsboro, Oregon but the world rages around us as recent events have shown. It has shown that now more than ever our understanding from where it was we came and where we are choosing to go does have an effect on our decision-making. How can we make good decisions about the future if we base our information on myths, convenient cozy stereotypes of ourselves and the people living around us?

East is not simply east and west is not simply west. That was the central truth that I learned out of my journey of self-discovery. I am east and west and many others are as well. Although, like any who over romanticize there own illusions of cultural superiority or purity for their comfortable views of the world, it often lacks the true low and base facts that every family of man has hanging in their closets. Nothing on this earth is pure and surely no man or society. We are all made bastards by our history.

When were there ever a "good old days" for African American slaves in this country or for Willamette Indians? Yet you hear some senior citizens pining for the good old days all the time. Good old days for whom and why were they so good for them? Clearly those who pine do not have a full picture of the past if so many others do not share the same perceptions. Like the Dali Lama pines for, my hope is that the future derives a more mature and deeper understanding of ourselves and the inherent good and evil in every society and man. Let us pine for the "good new days."

If we are to have good new days we certainly cannot forget or bury our past. If we do not like what we see we must at least recognize and endure the ugliness of it. Perhaps, as an NPR radio program alluded to in April of 2001, why so many Americans see Asians as foreign is due to the fact that they do not fit into the picture of what the "good old days" are supposed to be like. How many Americans can claim to have ever heard of the Chinese Exclusion Act enacted into law in 1882. Do they ever wonder why it is they felt so safe in neighborhoods built for their exclusion?

In the conclusion of this chapter is a verbatim copy of the immigration laws governing Chinese immigrants into the United States. Although the law is virtually unknown to Americans today, it illustrates the prevailing wisdom of its adopters at the time. The Act was not revoked until after World War II after many Chinese Americans had served in the American Armed forces. At the time of their service they may not have even enjoyed American citizenship. It explains why by 1924 the number of Chinese in the United States had dropped to fewer than 62,000. With no ability to marry and no prospects of owning property they crowded into Chinatowns for safety locked into a life of institutionalized slavery as many could not scratch out a living outside of their slums. Even this was not to the liking of mainstream society that dubbed Chinese as clan like, treacherous and exclusionary for gathering in numbers in their own little world instead of disbursing into the countryside where they could be easily subdued. Like American Indians, Chinese lived without rights up until recent history yet most Americans do not even consider Chinese to have suffered any of the racial obstacles that blacks or Mexicans have endured.

It is often perceived by whites and other minorities that the silent minority, Asians, have suffered little in terms of discrimination. In fact many do not even consider Asians to be a minority in the sense that African Americans and Mexican Americans are. The relatively small numbers and habitual lack of ability of Asians to band and provide a unified objection to their condition has added to the problem. According to a National Public Radio segment aired in Portland, Oregon on April 26, 2001, a survey of Americans revealed that over 1/3 question the loyalties of Chinese Americans. During the spy plane crisis in China in 2001 groups in American cities boycotted Chinese restaurants and some shouted, "send the Chinese to internment camps." According to an anti-defamation League Indexing system 25% of those polled responded very negatively to Chinese Americans and 40% somewhat negatively. The statistics were proclaimed to be alarming. Of course, it is no surprise to me. It has been the state of my life, everyday of my life. It has not diminished my love for the promise of America.

Further surveys of interest that were mentioned on the NPR radio piece were that Americans couldn't distinguish the difference between a Chinese American, Korean American, or a Japanese American. That means that a Taiwanese American spy working for the CIA can be stoned to death just as easily by mistake over anger toward China as a Chinese fighter pilot. Even an American Indian is not safe. These are not just hypothetical. In 1992 Vincent Chin was beaten to death in a hate crime that was blamed on domestic economic woes that were focused on the booming Japanese economy. Vincent was not Japanese as it turned out.

In 1885, 28 Chinese were killed in Rock Springs and in 1887, 31 Chinese miners were murdered in Northeast Oregon as whites vented over a similar economic post Civil War depression. Asians and to an even greater extent, Middle Easterners, are simply not understood by mainstream Americans. We have enough trouble sorting out our own history, yet sort it out we must, to move on. We still have a long way to go in understanding our neighbors in Hillsboro. If you are reading this right now ask yourself if you have ever heard of the Chinese Exclusion Act?

The following document enacted into law in 1882 during the Forty-Seventh Congress in Washington, D.C. speaks to the truth of our ignoble nature in the past and present. It is in all of us to be recognized.

The act was not revoked until 1943. The Walter-McCarran Act, passed in 1952, allowed first-generation Asian Americans to finally apply for U.S. citizenship. In 1965, the Immigration and Nationality Act eliminated blatant anti-Asian bias in U.S. immigration. To this day Chinese remain the only ethnic group specifically forbidden by law to enter the United States, a privilege not shared by any other ethnic group on earth.

Chinese Exclusion Act

Forty-Seventh Congress. Session I. 1882

Chapter 126.-An act to execute certain treaty stipulations relating to Chinese.

Preamble. Whereas, in the opinion of the Government of the United States the coming of Chinese laborers to this country endangers the good order of certain localities within the territory thereof:

Therefore,

Be it enacted by the Senate and House of Representatives of the United States of America in Congress assembled, That from and after the expiration of ninety days next after the passage of this act, and until the expiration of ten years next after the passage of this act, the coming of Chinese laborers to the United States be, and the same is hereby, suspended; and during such suspension it shall not be lawful for any Chinese laborer to come, or, having so come after the expiration of said ninety days, to remain within the United States.

SEC.2. That the master of any vessel who shall knowingly bring within the United States on such vessel, and land or permit to be landed, and Chinese laborer, from any foreign port of place, shall be deemed guilty of a misdemeanor, and on conviction thereof shall be punished by a fine of not more than five hundred dollars for each and every such Chinese laborer so brought, and may be also imprisoned for a term not exceeding one year.

SEC.3. That the two foregoing sections shall not apply to Chinese laborers who were in the United States on the seventeenth day of November, eighteen hundred and eighty, or who shall have come into the same before the expiration of ninety days next after the passage of this act, and who shall produce to such master before going on board such vessel, and shall produce to the collector of the port in the United States at which such vessel shall arrive, the evidence hereinafter in this act required of his being on of the laborers in this section mentioned; nor shall the two foregoing sections apply to the case of any master whose vessel, being bound to a port not within the United States by reason of being in distress or in stress of weather, or touching at any port of the United States on its voyage to any foreign port of place: Provided, That all Chinese laborers brought on such vessel shall depart with the vessel on leaving port.

SEC.4. That for the purpose of properly identifying Chinese laborers who were in the United States on the seventeenth day of November, eighteen hundred and eighty, or who shall have come into the same before the expiration of ninety days next after the passage of this act, and in order to furnish them with the proper evidence of their right to go from and come to the United States of their free will and accord, as provided by the treaty between the United States and China dated November Seventeenth, eighteen hundred and eighty, the collector of customs of the district from which any such Chinese laborer shall depart from the United States shall, in person or by deputy, go on board each vessel having on board any such Chinese laborer and cleared or about to sail from his district for a foreign port, and on such vessel make a list of all such Chinese laborers, which shall be entered in registry-books to be kept for that purpose, in which shall be stated the name, age, occupation, last place of residence, physical marks or peculiarities, and all facts necessary for the identification of each of such Chinese laborers, which books shall be safely kept in the custom-house; and every such Chinese laborer so departing from the United States shall be entitled to, and shall receive, free of any charge or cost upon application therefore, from the collector or his deputy, at the time such list is taken, a certificate, signed by the collector or his deputy and attested by this seal of office, in such form as the Secretary of the Treasury shall prescribe, which certificate shall contain a statement of the name, age, occupation, last place of residence, personal description, and fact of identification of the Chinese laborer to whom the certificate is issued, corresponding with the said list and registry in all particulars. In case any Chinese laborer after having received such certificate shall leave such vessel before her departure he shall deliver his certificate to the master of the vessel, and if such Chinese laborer shall fail to return to such vessel before her departure from port the certificate shall be delivered by the master to the collector of customs for cancellation. The certificate herein provided for shall entitle the Chinese laborer to whom the same is issued to return to and re-enter the United States upon producing and delivering the same to the collector of customs of the district at which such Chinese laborer shall seek to re-enter; and upon delivery of such certificate by such Chinese laborer to the collector of customs at the time or re-entry in the United States, said collector shall cause the same to be filed in the custom house and duly canceled.

SEC.5. That any Chinese laborer mentioned in section four of this act being in the United States, and desiring to depart from the United States by land, shall have the right to demand and receive, free of charge or cost, a certificate of indentification similar to that provided for in section four of this act to be issued to such Chinese laborers as may desire to leave the United States by water; and it is hereby made the duty of the collector of customs of the district next adjoining the foreign country to which said Chinese laborer desires to go to issue such certificate, free of charge or cost, upon application by such Chinese laborer, and to enter the same upon registry-books to be kept by him for the purpose, as provided for in section four of this act.

SEC.6. That in order to the faithful execution of articles one and two of the treaty in this act before mentioned, every Chinese person other than a laborer who may be entitled by said treaty and this act to come within the United States, and who shall be about to come to the United States, shall be identified as so entitled by the Chinese Government in each case, such identity to be evidenced by a certificate issued under the authority of said government, which certificate shall be in the English language or (if not in the English language) accompanied by a translation into English, stating such right to come, and which certificate shall state the name, title, or official rank, if any, the age, height, and all physical peculiarities, former an present occupation or profession, and place of residence in China of the person to whom the certificate is issued and that such person is entitled conformably to the treaty in this act mentioned to come within the United States. Such certificate shall be prima-facie evidence of the fact set forth therein, and shall be produced to the collector of customs, or his deputy, of the port in the district in the United States at which the person named therein shall arrive.

SEC.7. That any person who shall knowingly and falsely alter of substitute any name for the name written in such certificate or forge any such certificate, or knowingly utter any forged or fraudulent certificate, or falsely personate any person named in any such certificate, shall be deemed guilty of a misdemeanor; and upon conviction thereof shall be fined in a sum not exceeding one thousand dollars, an imprisoned in a penitentiary for a term of not more than five years.

SEC.8. That the master of any vessel arriving in the United States from any foreign port or place shall, at the same time he delivers a manifest of the cargo, and if there be no cargo, then at the time of making a report of the entry of vessel pursuant to the law, in addition to the other matter required to be reported, and before landing, or permitting to land, any Chinese passengers, deliver and report to the collector of customs of the district in which such vessels shall have arrived a separate list of all Chinese passengers taken on board his vessel at any foreign port or place, and all such passengers on board the vessel at that time. Such list shall show the names of such passengers (and if accredited officers of the Chinese Government traveling on the business of that government, or their servants, with a note of such facts), and the name and other particulars, as shown by their respective certificates; and such list shall be sworn to by the master in the manner required by law in relation to the manifest of the cargo. Any willful refusal or neglect of any such master to comply with the provisions of this section shall incur the same penalties and forfeiture as are provided for a refusal or neglect to report and deliver a manifest of cargo.

SEC.9. That before any Chinese passengers are landed from any such vessel, the collector, or his deputy, shall proceed to examine such passengers, comparing the certificates with the list and with the passengers; and no passenger shall be allowed to land in the United States from such vessel in violation of the law.

SEC.10. That every vessel whose master shall knowingly violated any of the provisions of this act shall be deemed forfeited to the United States, and shall be liable to seizure and condemnation on any district of the United States into which such vessel may enter or in which she may be found.

SEC.11. That any person who shall knowingly bring into or cause to be brought into the United States by land, or who shall knowingly aid or abet the same, or aid or abet the landing in the United States from any vessel of any Chinese person not lawfully entitled to enter the United States, shall be deemed guilty of a misdemeanor, and shall, on conviction thereof, be fined in a sum not exceeding one thousand dollars, and imprisoned for a term not exceeding one year.

SEC.12. That no Chinese person shall be permitted to enter the United States by land without producing to the proper officer of customs the certificate in this act required of Chinese persons seeking to land from a vessel. And any Chinese person found unlawfully within the United States shall be caused to be removed there from to the country from whence he came, by direction of the United States, after being brought before some justice, judge, or commissioner of a court of the United States and found to be one not lawfully entitled to be or remain in the United States.

SEC.13. That this act shall not apply to diplomatic and other officers of the Chinese Government traveling upon the business of that government, whose credentials shall be taken as equivalent to the certificate in this act mentioned, and shall exempt them and their body and household servants from the provisions of this act as to other Chinese persons.

SEC.14. That hereafter no State court or court of the United States shall admit Chinese to citizenship; and all laws in conflict with this act are hereby repealed.

SEC.15. that the words "Chinese laborers", whenever used in this act, shall be construed to mean both skilled and unskilled laborers and Chinese employed in mining.

Approved, May 6, 1882.

Notes

1. "Tension in Taiwan: The Polemics; China Denounces U.S. 'Interference' in Dispute With Taiwan," *NYT Archives Article On the Net*, March 22, 1996, by Seth Faison. Viewed 10/15/00.
2. "China's gambit to control Taiwan: China's military lacks resources to invade Taiwan," *Oregonian*, March 13, 2000, by Craig S. Smith-New York Times News Service.
3. "Tension in Taiwan: The Polemics; China Denounces U.S. 'Interference' in Dispute With Taiwan," *NYT Archives Article On the Net*, March 22, 1996, by Seth Faison. Viewed 10/15/00.
4. "'What Is China?' Taiwan's New Answer Is Puzzling," *NYT Archives On the Net*, July 14, 1999, by Seth Faison. Viewed 10/15/00.
5. "China's Leadership Pushes for Unity," *The New York Times On The Web*, March 9, 2001, by Erik Eckholm and Elisabeth Rosenthal. Viewed 3/9/01. www.nytimes.com/2001/03/09/world/09chin.html
6. Reid, Daniel P., Hans Hofer, *Insights Guides Taiwan.* (Singapore: APA Publications (HK) LTD, 1995).
7. Lin, Yutang, *The Wisdom Of Confucius.* (New York: The Modern Library, 1994).
8. Lin, April C.J., Jerome F. Keating. *Island In the Stream: A Quick Case Study of Taiwan's Complex History.* (Taipei: SMC Publishing Inc., 2000).
9. Reid, Daniel P., Hans Hofer, *Insights Guides Taiwan.* (Singapore: APA Publications (HK) LTD, 1995).
10. Lin, April C.J., Jerome F. Keating. *Island In the Stream: A Quick Case Study of Taiwan's Complex History.* (Taipei: SMC Publishing Inc., 2000).
11. Fairbanks, John King, and Merle Goldman. *China: A New History.*

(Cambridge, Massachusetts: The Belknap Press of Harvard University Press, 1998).

12. Lin, April C.J., Jerome F. Keating. *Island In the Stream: A Quick Case Study of Taiwan's Complex History.* (Taipei: SMC Publishing Inc., 2000).

13. Copper, John F. *Taiwan: Nation-State or Province?* Second Edition. (Taipei: SMC Publishing Inc., 1997).

14. Copper, John F. *Taiwan: Nation-State or Province?* Second Edition. (Taipei: SMC Publishing Inc., 1997).

15. Reid, Daniel P., Hans Hofer, *Insights Guides Taiwan.* (Singapore: APA Publications (HK) LTD, 1995).

16. "Taiwan's 400 years of history," *Ilha Formosa Website,* Viewed 11/19/99, www.taiwandc.org/hst-1624.htm

17. Lin, Yutang, *The Wisdom Of Confucius.* (New York: The Modern Library, 1994).

18. Lin, Yutang, *The Wisdom Of Confucius.* (New York: The Modern Library, 1994).

19. Copper, John F. *Taiwan: Nation-State or Province?* Second Edition. (Taipei: SMC Publishing Inc., 1997).

20. Fairbanks, John King, and Merle Goldman. *China: A New History.* (Cambridge, Massachusetts: The Belknap Press of Harvard University Press, 1998).

21. Copper, John F. *Taiwan: Nation-State or Province?* Second Edition. (Taipei: SMC Publishing Inc., 1997).

22. Copper, John F. *Taiwan: Nation-State or Province?* Second Edition. (Taipei: SMC Publishing Inc., 1997).

23. Reid, Daniel P., Hans Hofer, *Insights Guides Taiwan.* (Singapore: APA Publications (HK) LTD, 1995).

24. Reid, Daniel P., Hans Hofer, *Insights Guides Taiwan.* (Singapore: APA Publications (HK) LTD, 1995).

25. Copper, John F. *Taiwan: Nation-State or Province?* Second Edition. (Taipei: SMC Publishing Inc., 1997).

26. Lin, April C.J., Jerome F. Keating. *Island In the Stream: A Quick Case Study of Taiwan's Complex History.* (Taipei: SMC Publishing Inc., 2000).

27. Copper, John F. *Taiwan: Nation-State or Province?* Second Edition. (Taipei: SMC Publishing Inc., 1997).

28. Reid, Daniel P., Hans Hofer, *Insights Guides Taiwan.* (Singapore: APA Publications (HK) LTD, 1995).

29. Copper, John F. *Taiwan: Nation-State or Province?* Second Edition. (Taipei: SMC Publishing Inc., 1997).

30. Lin, April C.J., Jerome F. Keating. *Island In the Stream: A Quick Case Study of Taiwan's Complex History.* (Taipei: SMC Publishing Inc., 2000).

31. Copper, John F. *Taiwan: Nation-State or Province?* Second Edition. (Taipei: SMC Publishing Inc., 1997).

32. "Taiwan President Implies His Island Is Sovereign State," *NYT Archives Article On the Net,* July 14, 1999, by Seth Faison. Viewed 10/15/00.

33. "'What Is China?' Taiwan's New Answer Is Puzzling," *NYT Archives On the Net,* July 14, 1999, by Seth Faison. Viewed 10/15/00.

34. "Taiwan's 400 years of history," *Ilha Formosa Website,* Viewed 11/19/99, www.taiwandc.org/hst-1624.htm

35. Copper, John F. *Taiwan: Nation-State or Province?* Second Edition. (Taipei: SMC Publishing Inc., 1997).

36. "Taiwan's 400 years of history," *Ilha Formosa Website,* Viewed 11/19/99, www.taiwandc.org/hst-1624.htm

37. "Taiwan's 400 years of history," *Ilha Formosa Website,* Viewed 11/19/99, www.taiwandc.org/hst-1624.htm

38. Copper, John F. *Taiwan: Nation-State or Province?* Second Edition. (Taipei: SMC Publishing Inc., 1997).

39. Copper, John F. *Taiwan: Nation-State or Province?* Second Edition. (Taipei: SMC Publishing Inc., 1997).

40. Evans, Karin, *The Lost Daughters Of China.* (New York: Jeremy P. Tarcher/Putnam., 2000).

41. Evans, Karin, *The Lost Daughters Of China.* (New York: Jeremy P. Tarcher/Putnam., 2000).

42. Lin, April C.J., Jerome F. Keating. *Island In the Stream: A Quick Case Study of Taiwan's Complex History.* (Taipei: SMC Publishing Inc., 2000).

43. Copper, John F. *Taiwan: Nation-State or Province?* Second Edition. (Taipei: SMC Publishing Inc., 1997).

44. Lin, April C.J., Jerome F. Keating. *Island In the Stream: A Quick Case Study of Taiwan's Complex History.* (Taipei: SMC Publishing Inc., 2000).

45. "The *forgotten* prison," *Taipei Times Online,* November 28, 1999, by Mike Clendeuin. Viewed 12/3/99.
www.taipeitimes.com/news/1999/11/28/story/0000012822

46. "The *forgotten* prison," *Taipei Times Online,* November 28, 1999, by Mike Clendeuin. Viewed 12/3/99.
www.taipeitimes.com/news/1999/11/28/story/0000012822

47. "The *forgotten* prison," *Taipei Times Online,* November 28, 1999, by Mike Clendeuin. Viewed   12/3/99.
www.taipeitimes.com/news/1999/11/28/story/0000012822

48. Copper, John F. *Taiwan: Nation-State or Province?* Second Edition. (Taipei: SMC Publishing Inc., 1997).
49. Copper, John F. *Taiwan: Nation-State or Province?* Second Edition. (Taipei: SMC Publishing Inc., 1997).
50. "Background Notes: Taiwan, August 1999," Released by the Bureau of East Asian and Pacific Affairs U.S. Department of State. Viewed 10/16/00. www.state.gov/www/background_notes/taiwan_899_bgn.html
51. "History of Little League," *Sporting News.* Viewed 4/10/01. tsn.sportingnews.com/archives/littleleague/champions.html
52. Copper, John F. *Taiwan: Nation-State or Province?* Second Edition. (Taipei: SMC Publishing Inc., 1997).
53. "EERI Special Earthquake Report - December 1999. The Chi-Chi, Taiwan Earthquake of September 21, 1999," Earthquake Engineering Research Institute. Viewed 1/24/01. www.eeri.org/reconn/Taiwan1299/TaiwanFinal.html
54. "A Tale of Taiwan's Wildlife From "New Species" to "Endangered Species"," Viewed 1/25/01. www.sinorama.comtw/8504/504006e1.html
55. "A Tale of Taiwan's Wildlife From "New Species" to "Endangered Species"," Viewed 1/25/01. www.sinorama.comtw/8504/504006e1.html
56. "A Tale of Taiwan's Wildlife From "New Species" to "Endangered Species"," Viewed 1/25/01. www.sinorama.comtw/8504/504006e1.html
57. "A Tale of Taiwan's Wildlife From "New Species" to "Endangered Species"," Viewed 1/25/01. www.sinorama.comtw/8504/504006e1.html
58. "Environmental assessments requires impact," *Taipei Times Online,* April 9, 2000, by Lin Sue. Viewed 1/25/01. www.taipeitimes.com/news/2000/04/09/story/0000031622
59. "A Tale of Taiwan's Wildlife From "New Species" to "Endangered Species"," Viewed 1/25/01. www.sinorama.comtw/8504/504006e1.html
60. "Investigation of Nature Sancturary (Reserve) in Taiwan," Viewed 1/25/01. www.bird.org.tw/English/Conservation/ereserve.html
61. "Environmental assessments requires impact," *Taipei Times Online,* April 9, 2000, by Lin Sue. Viewed 1/25/01. www.taipeitimes.com/news/2000/04/09/story/0000031622
62. Lin, Yutang, *The Wisdom Of Confucius.* (New York: The Modern Library, 1994).